3/09

3/09

PINTXOS

PINTXOS

SMALL PLATES in the BASQUE TRADITION

GERALD HIRIGOYEN

with Lisa Weiss

PHOTOGRAPHY BY MAREN CARUSO

TEN SPEED PRESS
Berkeley | Toronto

Ten Speed Press
PO Box 7123
Berkeley, California 94707
www.tenspeed.com

Distributed in Australia by Simon and Schuster Australia, in Canada by
Ten Speed Press Canada, in New Zealand by Southern Publishers Group,
in South Africa by Real Books, and in the United Kingdom and Europe by
Publishers Group UK.

Cover and text design by Katy Brown
Food styling by Kim Kissling
Prop styling by Christine Wolheim

Library of Congress Cataloging-in-Publication Data
Hirigoyen, Gerald.
   Pintxos : small plates in the Basque tradition / Gerald Hirigoyen
with Lisa Weiss ; photography by Maren Caruso.
       p. cm.
   Includes index.
   ISBN-13: 978-1-58008-922-7 (hardcover with jacket)
   ISBN-10: 1-58008-922-4 (hardcover with jacket)
   1. Tapas. 2. Cookery, Basque. 3. Cookery, American—California style.
I. Weiss, Lisa, 1951- II. Title.
   TX740.H566 2009
   641.8'12—dc22

                              2008043518

Printed in China
First printing, 2009

1 2 3 4 5 6 7 8 9 10 – 13 12 11 10 09

CONTENTS

INTRODUCTION

Even as a kid I enjoyed *ir de tapeo*, or the tradition of going from one tapas bar to the next, in San Sebastián with my parents and their friends. In my earliest memories of those days, I first see a wall of legs on a floor littered with sawdust, toothpicks, cigarette butts, and shrimp shells, and then my father sweeps me up so I can sample from the awesome display of food on the bar. When I was older and seated at a table in a restaurant, I chafed at having to mind my manners and to wait for each course to arrive, but at the tapas bars I was free. I could take anything I wanted from the platters of child-sized portions—maybe a piece of chorizo, a square of *tortilla española*, or a hard-boiled egg, along with a Fanta soda—and run off down the street to play with my sister and the other children, before catching up with my parents at the next *tasca* (tavern).

My sense of taste is at full strength only when standing up.
—CALVIN TRILLIN

I still like the freedom from formal dining that tapas bars offer, though now as an adult I also appreciate them for their conviviality—as places where people from all walks of life can get together for lively conversation, a glass of wine, and premeal, postmeal, or even full-meal bites.

In Spain, tapas specialties vary from region to region and are commonly eaten with knife and fork while seated at a counter. In the Basque region, where I grew up, tapas are known as *pintxos*, the Basque spelling (pronounced PEEN-chos), or *pinchos* in Spanish (from the word *pinchar*, which means "to skewer") and are typically finger foods eaten in one or two bites while standing up. Indeed, the tapas tradition is so strong in the Basque Country that a hard-fought competition, complete with strict rules defining the size of the *pintxos*, is held annually.

Some *pintxos* are quite basic, maybe just some cubes of chorizo or cheese on tooth-picks. Others are more elaborate, such as small sandwiches (*bocadillos*), plates of fried seafood (*fritos*), or little earthenware dishes (*cazuelitas*) of various braises (*estofados*). And always in San Sebastián you will find creative bite-size combinations of meat, cheese, vegetables, and/or fruit, either threaded onto skewers (*pintxos*) or placed on top of small slices of bread (*montaditos*). But whether you call them by their Spanish name *tapas* or Basque name *pintxos*, it is the casual way they are served that makes these small plates synonymous with a relaxed, fun-filled atmosphere.

Even though informality and spontaneity are the hallmarks of a good tapas bar, the food they serve is taken seriously, and every bar has its specialty or specialties. I can't count the number of times I have been involved in an intense discussion of politics or soc-cer while sipping Txacolí (a mildly effervescent Basque wine), only to have to stop and say "My God, that *pintxo* is good!" Of course, many cultures have their little dishes, such as Greek meze, Cantonese dim sum, and Italian antipasti, but the Spanish have turned the concept of small plates into both a social event and a culinary art form.

Spaniards still like to debate the origin of the tapa, but most agree that the first tapas were created in Andalusia to serve a practical purpose: to keep flies out of glasses of sherry. Tapa means "lid" and is derived from the word *tapar*, "to cover," so the common-sense theory is that tavern owners would drape a slice of ham or cheese or place a small plate of olives or almonds on top of a glass to create a barrier against bugs. Eventually, the bars with the better "covers" began attracting more customers, and a competition soon developed among owners to see who could create the tastiest tidbits. Not surpris-ingly, patrons began to move from one bar to the next to sample their offerings. Tapas also served two other seemingly contradictory functions: a few salty nibbles not only increased patrons' thirst for more wine, but also helped to keep them from getting drunk, a serious transgression in polite Spanish society.

It is ironic that from such humble beginnings an entire culture—a kind of traveling street party—has been created around the bars that serve tapas, and food that was once so simple has become, in many cases, not only baroque but also frequently global. This is par-ticularly true in San Sebastián, a popular resort city, where some of the most delicious, and in recent years, innovative tapas have been created. Although San Sebastián still harbors old-school tapas made from unique Spanish ingredients, such as marinated *boquerones* (anchovies) or slices of *serrano* ham cured by the tapas bar owner's wife, I now often find myself shaking my head in wonder at the elaborately stacked, decorated, and skewered *pintxos* fashioned from foie gras from France, balsamic vinegar from Modena, or smoked salmon from Norway. Some of these tapas are miniature culinary works of art, influenced by the *nueva cucina* revolution in Spain, and although the chef in me admires the cutting-edge creativity now happening in my homeland, I must confess that the small dishes I crave are the simple ones, the ones that I loved as a child: a piece of *bacalao* (salt cod) on a toasted baguette slice, or some calamari quickly seared *a la plancha*.

After I returned to California from a trip to San Sebastián in 2003, I couldn't stop thinking about all the wonderful food I had enjoyed there, particularly the seafood, which is arguably the best in the world, and the *pintxos*, both traditional and contemporary. That trip convinced me that it was the right time for me to open a true tapas bar in San Francisco.

When I opened Bocadillos in 2004, I had a clear and simple vision in mind: For selfish reasons, I wanted to create the kind of place where I could go with friends to enjoy a glass or two of wine and a few delicious nibbles. I also wanted a space that allowed me to indulge my passion for the foods and style of eating I loved. That meant it had to be a Spanish-styled tapas bar, as authentic as possible, using mainly fresh local ingredients and incorporating some global culinary influences. After all, I have lived in California for most of my adult life and have broadened the scope of my cooking. Today, Bocadillos has evolved into my kind of place. It's informal and comfortable, and serves food that is true to my Basque culinary heritage, yet incorporates the ingredients and culinary influences of California. Our wine list, made up mostly of Spanish, Basque, and California bottles, complements the food.

About three years after opening Bocadillos, I came home from an afternoon of bike riding to find that my wife, Cameron, had invited a few friends over for an impromptu Sunday dinner. What to do? Quickly I searched the pantry and discovered the makings of a tapas party. I had a couple of cans of *ventresca* tuna and some *piquillo* peppers. In the refrigerator, next to a leftover beet salad from the night before, was a piece of *serrano* ham and some greens from the farmers' market, along with a chunk of Idiazábal cheese and a jar of Spanish olives. I drove to the store and picked up fresh bread and lamb chops. Within an hour, our guests were gathering around the kitchen island and I was serving them wine and the sliced ham, olives, and cheese. As everyone was getting happy from the wine and finger food, I stuffed the peppers with the tuna, grilled the lamb, and tossed the beets with the greens. Finally and barely breaking a sweat, I put out the finished dishes, along with some small plates and flatware, and then I let my guests help themselves.

That evening's menu was the genesis of this book. Maybe because I own two restaurants in San Francisco, friends assume that I must be eating "gourmet" meals every night. But the truth is that I feel lucky on the rare occasion when I can even join my family for dinner during the week, and our weekends are so jam-packed with soccer games and my restaurant events that entertaining has become a luxury. I realized that the dishes I serve at Bocadillos and, in smaller portions, the food from Pipérade, my Basque restaurant, is what I like to serve at home for casual occasions. And it is easy to do. You need only to buy some good charcuterie and cheese, open a can or jar, and make one or two braised or grilled dishes and a salad and you will have a no-fuss, fast-to-assemble dinner for four, six, eight, or more.

What you will find in the pages that follow are recipes for the small-plate dishes I make at my restaurants that can be prepared quickly and easily at home. What you won't find are complicated chef's recipes—okay, I admit to a couple of exceptions—with lots of steps and obscure ingredients. In the years that have passed since I wrote *The Basque Kitchen* in 1999, ingredients that were once difficult to obtain, such as *serrano* ham, smoked paprika, *piment d'Espelette*, and Basque sheep's milk cheeses, have become almost commonplace in better food markets and are easy to buy online.

The chapters in the book are organized to roughly parallel the Bocadillos menu, with recipes divided primarily into categories by technique, presentation, or ingredients. I begin with A La Plancha, an age-old Spanish method—particularly popular in the Basque region—in which meats and seafood are seared on a hot griddle (traditionally a cast-iron plate placed over a wood fire). The two other technique-based chapters are Estofados, which includes stews and braises, and Fritos, the crispy fried bites that are invariably the first to disappear from the table. Ingredient-based chapters are Habas, which features fresh and dried shelling beans, staples of the Basque diet, and Organos, which is called the Innard Circle on the Bocadillos menu. The Spanish have long treasured the parts of the animal that many Americans discard, but I have noticed that more and more of our customers are trying innards, and I have included the recipes for the most popular dishes at the restaurant. Ensaladas and Sopas, or salads and soups, are not traditional tapas, but they reflect the influence California has had on my cooking. The remaining three chapters are my favorites: Pintxos and Montaditos, or tapas on skewers and tapas on bread, and Bocadillos, or little sandwiches. Finally, you'll find a Pantry chapter, which is a glossary of basic ingredients and preparations you'll need to stock your kitchen to prepare dishes from the book.

When planning a menu, keep in mind that all of the recipes are flexible. Most of them can be made ahead of time, many are served at room temperature, and quantities can often be increased or decreased to suit the size of your group. Also, many of the recipes can do double duty as hors d'oeuvres. For a tapas spread, I suggest choosing one recipe from five or six different chapters, perhaps an *a la plancha* dish, a braise, a salad, a soup, a *pintxo*, and a *frito*, or you can also select one of your own favorite recipes and turn it into a tapa, using my recipes for inspiration.

This book is about my kind of soul food. It is about the foods I grew up with and the foods I have cooked over the years. It is about real ingredients and authentic flavors. Most of all it is about breaking bread and clinking glasses with the people you love. So in the true spirit of *ir de tapeo*, I urge you to invite some friends over, choose a few recipes, go to the store, and get in the kitchen. Then before you know it, you will have a party. Oh, and don't forget to open the wine. Hopefully, you will have done that already.

ABOUT WINE

The wine-pairing suggestions that accompany recipes in this book are limited to wines from Spain, the Basque Country of Spain and France, and California. Many incredible wines are now being produced in wine-growing regions around the world, so why the exclusivity? The answer is a venerable culinary axiom: what grows together goes together. It is a sound philosophy not only for matching foods, such as fava beans and asparagus, or beets and potatoes, but also for matching foods with wines. Think of foie gras with Sauternes, Bolognese sauce with Sangiovese di Romana, and, of course, tapas with sherry. The wines from Spain and the Basque Country are natural matches with the gutsy, flavorful ingredients that go into all of my dishes. And because the agricultural riches of my adopted home continue to inspire me with new ideas in the kitchen, California wines and my recipes are an equally felicitous marriage.

Spaniards have always enjoyed wine, drinking it with nearly every meal—sometimes even taking a sip of sherry after breakfast. Thanks to the British, sherry has enjoyed centuries of worldwide recognition, but few other Spanish wines have matched that glory, other than the red wines of Rioja and the *cavas*, or sparkling wines, of Catalonia. Historically, the rough, high-alcohol reds and low-acid whites of Spain were drunk—and appreciated—only by the Spanish.

But in the mid-nineteenth century, when phylloxera devastated many of their vineyards, French vintners began migrating to Spain, where they planted grapes, mainly in the areas of Navarre, Rioja, and Catalonia, and introduced more modern production techniques. Slowly the quality of Spanish wine began to improve, only to have the political turmoil of the twentieth century bring progress almost to a halt. However, with the death of dictator Francisco Franco in 1975, which ended nearly four decades of iron-fisted rule, Spain began the transition to democracy, and Spanish vintners once again set about improving the quality of their wines.

Today, Spain is the third largest wine producer in the world, behind France and Italy, with the United States fourth. Of course, marvelous wines are being made in every corner of the country, but the Basque region, with its three historical provinces in France (Labourd, Lower Navarre, and Soule) and four historical provinces in Spain (Biscay, Gipuzkoa, Araba, and Navarre), is an up and coming player on the world wine stage. The most notable wines from the Spanish side are the classic Rioja Tempranillos, the wines of Navarre (especially those made from the Garnacha grape), and the sprightly Txacolí, made just outside San Sebastián. The French side offers robust alternatives with its white and red Irouléguy wines. The best wines of Spain have an appellation designation, or DO (*Denominación de Origen*), of which there are currently sixty-six, and there are two regions, Rioja and Priorat, that have a higher designation, DOCa (*Denominación de Origen Calificada*).

The U.S. wine industry has also come a long way in recent decades. In 1970, California was home to only 110 bonded wineries. Today, there are more than 1,300, and the state is the fifth largest wine producer in the world, with almost 1 million acres of vineyards. Much of that land is planted with familiar classic French varieties, such as Cabernet Sauvignon, Pinot Noir, and Chardonnay, but California vintners are also experimenting with grapes from every corner of the globe, such as Tempranillo from Spain or Gruner Veltliner from Austria. Not all of these experiments yield outstanding results, but they do reflect an American idealism that encourages trying new things—an idealism that has advanced the California wine industry in a relatively short amount of time and has produced a diverse array of wines along the way.

When you are selecting a wine, your choice is often in large part subjective, and is influenced by where you are dining, whom you are dining with, and your state of mind (in love, stressed out, tired). Sommeliers, in contrast, typically consider just three primary factors, all less subjective, when determining the best wine: the taste, smell, and feel of the food.

At the end of most of the recipes in this book, you will see a brief section titled To Drink that includes one or more Spanish, Basque, and/or Californian wines, selected according to a sommelier's three primary considerations for pairing. The exceptions are the recipes in the Pinchos and Montaditos chapters. It is customary throughout Spain to pair these small plates, which are typically no more than one or two bites, with wines that are versatile enough to mate well with a variety of foods. That's because customers are moving almost constantly from one plate to the next, from one flavor to another. Manzanilla and fino sherries from Jerez, rosés from Rioja and Navarre, and Txacolí from the Basque County are the most popular choices with these dishes.

Use the wine-pairing recommendations as guidelines to help you pick out a wine at the wine shop or from your wine rack. Although a specific winery is often named, it is not because it is the only one that makes a compatible wine. Instead, consider the winery as a starting point to finding a similar wine. To that end, a simple legend identifying the wine qualities that make a good match has been included with each recommendation. That means that you can walk into any wine store and ask, "Do you have a Claiborne & Churchill Riesling? And if not, what would you recommend that is medium bodied, dry, and fruity?"

L	Light bodied or delicate
M	Medium bodied
B	Bold or full bodied
D	Dry or lacking any apparent sweetness
F	Fruity*

*You must distinguish between fruity and the sensation of fruit and sweetness, which refers to the residual sugar in the wine. In other words, a wine that is fruity can also be dry.

A LA PLANCHA
on the griddle

PRAWNS with GARLIC CHIPS and PRESERVED LEMON

Over the years, I have learned that most Americans prefer their shrimp shelled. But the shells add lots of good flavor and help protect the shellfish from overcooking. If you can find head-on prawns for this dish, you will have the added bonus of being able to suck on the heads to get every last morsel of tasty meat. Yes, the job of shelling them at the table can be messy, but here the shell is split and the dark intestinal vein removed before they are cooked, eliminating some of the diners' work. Provide your guests plenty of napkins, and serve crusty bread to soak up the juices. **Serves 4**

12 large prawns (16/20 count) with shell and head intact (about ¾ pound total)

2 tablespoons olive oil

¼ teaspoon piment d'Espelette (see page 179)

Fleur de sel or other coarse salt for finishing

1 tablespoon Garlic Chips (page 178)

1 teaspoon finely diced Confit of Lemon (page 176)

1 teaspoon finely chopped fresh flat-leaf parsley

Using small scissors or a paring knife, and working on the convex side (opposite the legs), cut along the length of each prawn shell, leaving the head and tail intact. Remove and discard the dark veinlike intestinal tract.

Heat a griddle, cast-iron skillet, or sauté pan over medium-high heat. Add 1 tablespoon of the olive oil and warm it until it ripples. (If you have just made the garlic chips, use the garlic-flavored oil remaining in the pan to cook the prawns.) Add the prawns and cook on the first side for about 2 minutes, or until they begin to turn opaque. Using tongs, turn and cook on the second side for about 2 minutes, or until bright pink and opaque.

To serve, immediately transfer the prawns to a warmed plate and sprinkle with the piment d'Espelette, fleur de sel to taste, garlic chips, lemon confit, and parsley. Drizzle the remaining 1 tablespoon olive oil over the shrimp and toss well.

TO DRINK

White Riojas, though not as widely available as red ones, are food-friendly wines. The prawns call for a medium-bodied, round wine, but with a bright, fresh acidity to complement the preserved lemon. Look for a white Rioja from Remelluri. You will pay a handsome price, but you will be rewarded with what some consider Spain's finest white. **M D**

CALAMARI with PEPPERS
and WILD MUSHROOM SALAD

I cook calamari—squid—often, usually quickly on a hot griddle, as I do here. Or sometimes I give them a brief dunk in boiling water and use them in a salad, or I stuff and braise them. You are likely to find cleaned squid at your fish market, already separated into tubes and tentacles and skinned, but for this recipe I suggest you clean your own so you can keep the mottled purplish gray skin on the tubes. When the calamari is grilled, the skin adds flavor and makes a more striking presentation. Skin on or off, always keep in mind what I call the three- or thirty-minute calamari cooking rule: to prevent it from becoming rubbery, cook it very quickly, three minutes or less, or cook it for a long time, thirty minutes or more.   **Serves 4**

3 tablespoons olive oil

6 cups cleaned wild mushrooms, (about ¾ pound), cut into bite-size pieces if large

2 red bell peppers, cored, seeded, and sliced lengthwise ¼ inch thick

1 poblano chile, cored, seeded, and sliced lengthwise ¼ inch thick

¼ cup Pedro Ximénez sweet sherry

Kosher salt and freshly ground black pepper

1 pound whole calamari, cleaned (see page 175), or ¾ pound cleaned calamari, whole tubes and tentacles, preferably skin on

VINAIGRETTE

3 tablespoons sherry vinegar

1 tablespoon Pedro Ximénez sweet sherry

1 tablespoon extra virgin olive oil

1 cup loosely packed fresh flat-leaf parsley leaves

Piment d'Espelette (see page 179)

Fleur de sel or other coarse salt

Heat a large sauté pan over high heat until very hot. Add 2 tablespoons of the olive oil and warm the oil until it ripples. Add the mushrooms and cook, without stirring, for 1 minute. Then cook, stirring, for 1 to 2 minutes longer, or until lightly browned. Add the bell peppers and chile and cook for 1 minute longer. Add the sherry and stir to scrape up the browned bits on the bottom of the pan and let cook for a few seconds to evaporate some of the sherry. Season with salt and pepper and transfer to a bowl. Let cool to room temperature.

In a bowl, toss the calamari with the remaining 1 tablespoon olive oil and a little salt. Heat a griddle, cast-iron skillet, or sauté pan over medium-high heat until very hot. Using tongs, add the calamari and cook on the first side for 30 seconds, or until lightly browned. Turn and cook on the second side for 20 seconds, or until lightly browned. Transfer to a plate and let cool to room temperature.

To make the vinaigrette, in a small bowl, whisk together the sherry vinegar, sherry, and olive oil.

CONTINUED

Calamari with Peppers and Wild Mushroom Salad, *continued*

To serve, add about ¾ cup of the parsley to the peppers and mushrooms and toss to mix. Transfer to a rimmed platter or plate. Top with the calamari, and strew the platter with the remaining ¼ cup parsley leaves. Drizzle the vinaigrette over all, and sprinkle the calamari with a little piment d'Espelette and fleur de sel.

TO DRINK

Be daring here. This is a quintessential tapa, full of flavor from the calamari, mushrooms, and poblano chile. Try an amontillado sherry, a fortified wine that is dry, mildly nutty, and slightly acidic. Another choice, if you can find it, is the much sought-after and ethereal palo cortado, which begins its evolution as a fino but loses its yeast (flor) and develops the dark, rich, and nutty flavor of an oloroso yet retains the tangy characteristic of a fino. **B D**

HANGER STEAK with CHIMICHURRI

My father used to make what he called simply "herb sauce," which I later learned was similar to the well-known Argentinean salsa chimichurri. Many countries have their own version of this condiment; the common ingredient is fresh oregano, which marries particularly well with steak. If you make the sauce ahead, hold out the vinegar until just before serving, so the herbs remain brightly colored. Chimichurri is also terrific with all kinds of fish, shellfish, and poultry. If you like spice, add a pinch of red pepper flakes or minced jalapeño chile. ✂ **Serves 4**

CHIMICHURRI SAUCE

2 tablespoons finely chopped fresh chives

1½ tablespoons finely chopped shallot

2½ tablespoons coarsely chopped fresh flat-leaf parsley

1 tablespoon coarsely chopped fresh oregano

3 tablespoons sherry vinegar

1 tablespoon extra virgin olive oil

Kosher salt and freshly ground black pepper

Red pepper flakes or minced jalapeño chile (optional)

1 hanger steak or flank steak, about ¾ pound

Kosher salt and freshly ground black pepper

2 tablespoons olive oil

Preheat the oven to 475°F.

To make the sauce, in a small bowl, stir together the chives, shallot, parsley, oregano, sherry vinegar, and olive oil. Season to taste with salt, pepper, and red pepper flakes. Set aside.

Season the steak generously on both sides with salt and pepper. Heat a griddle, cast-iron skillet, or sauté pan over medium-high heat until hot. Add the olive oil and warm it until it ripples. Add the steak and cook on the first side for about 1 minute, or until lightly browned. Using tongs, turn and cook on the second side for 1 minute more, or until lightly browned. Transfer the pan to the oven and cook for about 3 minutes, or until an instant-read thermometer inserted into the center of the steak registers 125°F (because of the thinness of the meat, you can also make a discreet cut with a small knife to check), or to desired doneness. Transfer the meat to a cutting board and let rest for 3 to 4 minutes.

To serve, slice the steak across the grain on the diagonal into ½-inch-thick strips. Arrange the strips on a warmed platter, and drizzle with the sauce.

TO DRINK

Steak with a complex sauce like chimichurri calls for a bold, rustic Basque red. Irouléguy comes to mind, especially wines from Domaine Etxegaraya or Domaine Arretxea because they are loaded with luscious black fruit, acid, and vigorous tannins—all perfect for meat. **B D F**

DUCK BREAST with ORANGES
and GREEN OLIVES

For me, oranges and olives represent the essence of Spanish cuisine. Here, they are combined with duck in a dish reminiscent of the French duck à l'orange, so I have dubbed it duck à l'espagnole. I prefer Muscovy duck breasts, which are available at specialty butchers and by mail order (see Sources). They are lean and have a definite meaty but not-too-gamey flavor, and because they are fairly small, they cook quickly on a hot griddle. Pekin (Long Island) duck breasts are fine, too. Use a good, rich homemade or commercial stock here; canned chicken broth simply won't do. **Serves 4**

2 large navel oranges

1 tablespoon Grand Marnier

3 tablespoons plus 1 teaspoon sherry vinegar

1½ tablespoons sugar

3 tablespoons homemade Dark Chicken Stock (page 176), Veal Stock (page 185), or good-quality commercial chicken or veal stock (see Sources)

6 to 8 Arbequina or Manzanillo olives, pitted and slivered lengthwise

Kosher salt and freshly ground pepper

2 boneless Muscovy or Pekin duck breast halves (about ½ pound each)

2 tablespoons unsalted butter

Using a vegetable peeler, remove the zest from 1 orange in 2-inch-long pieces, leaving the white pith on the orange. Set the zest aside. Halve the orange and juice it into a small saucepan (you should have about ⅓ cup juice). Bring the orange juice to a boil over high heat, reduce the heat to medium, and add the Grand Marnier, 3 tablespoons of the sherry vinegar, and the sugar. Simmer, stirring occasionally, for 1 to 2 minutes, or until the sugar dissolves. Increase the heat to medium-high and cook for about 3 minutes, or until the liquid is reduced by half and is thick and syrupy. Add the stock and reduce the liquid to about ¼ cup. Add the olives and season with salt and pepper. Remove from the heat and set aside. (The sauce can be made up to 2 hours in advance, covered, and reserved at room temperature.)

Cut the reserved zest into strips ⅛ inch wide. Bring a small saucepan filled with water to a boil, add the zest strips, and blanch for 1 minute. Drain in a sieve, rinse with cold running water, and set the zest aside.

Cut a slice off of the top and bottom of the remaining orange to expose the flesh. With the orange standing upright, slice off the peel in wide strips, following the contour of the fruit and removing all of the white pith. Holding the orange in one hand over a bowl, cut along both sides of each segment, freeing the segments from the membrane and letting them drop into the bowl. Set the segments aside.

Using a sharp knife, score the skin of the duck breasts in a ½-inch crosshatch pattern, being careful not to cut through to the flesh. Heat a griddle, cast-iron skillet, or sauté pan over medium-high heat until very hot. Add the duck breasts, skin side down, and cook for 4 minutes, or until the skin is golden. Using tongs, turn and cook on the second side for 4 minutes. Turn a final time and cook skin side down for 2 minutes (the duck should still be pink in the center if you make a discreet cut to check). Transfer the duck breasts to a cutting board and let rest for 5 minutes before slicing.

To serve, reheat the sauce over medium-high heat and swirl in the butter until melted. Taste and adjust the seasoning with salt and pepper if necessary, and add the remaining 1 teaspoon vinegar to brighten the flavor. Add the orange segments and stir to coat.

Holding a knife almost parallel to the cutting board, cut the duck breasts into ¾-inch-wide slices. Fan the slices on a warmed rimmed platter or plate. Spoon the sauce over the top and strew with the orange zest.

TO DRINK

Pair an old-style Rioja red, something with delicacy and finesse as well as structure and tannin—Muga Prado Enea and La Rioja Alta Gran Reserva are two good choices—with this dish inspired by a French classic. **M D**

PORK MEDALLIONS CONFIT with CURRIED APPLE and CELERY ROOT SALAD

The word *confit*, which traditionally refers to an old-fashioned method of slowly cooking a salted and seasoned meat (most commonly duck or goose) in its own fat, has developed a certain cachet on American restaurant menus. Diners now recognize that a meat identified as a confit will not only be flavorful, but will also have a tender interior and a crispy exterior, and be surprisingly grease free. Meats that take well to this process are usually those with a high proportion of fat, such as duck, but almost any meat can be cooked in fat with wonderful results. In this recipe, I use pork tenderloin, a lean cut, cook it in duck fat, chill it, and then quickly sear thinly sliced pieces a la plancha. I serve the pork confit with a "lean and clean" riff on céleri-rave rémoulade, a dressing of celery root and apple, with a light curry vinaigrette instead of the traditional mayonnaise-based sauce.

Although you can cook the pork in olive oil, I recommend duck fat, which will give the meat an incomparable flavor and texture. It's available in well-stocked markets and online (see Sources). Once the meat is eaten, you can strain the fat, refrigerate it, and reuse it for another confit or for cooking astonishingly delicious fried potatoes. ❧ **Serves 4**

1 pound pork tenderloin

2 teaspoons kosher salt

1 tablespoon olive oil

1 tablespoon black peppercorns

1 tablespoon coriander seed

1 bay leaf

3 or 4 sprigs thyme

1 head garlic, halved crosswise

3 to 4 cups duck fat (see Sources) warmed to a liquid state, or olive oil

Cut the pork into 2 or 3 pieces that will fit snugly in a 1-quart resealable plastic bag. Sprinkle the pork pieces with the salt and put them into the bag with the peppercorns, coriander, and bay leaf, rubbing the spices into the meat as needed to distribute them evenly. Add the thyme and garlic, seal the bag, and refrigerate for at least 8 hours or up to overnight.

To cook the pork, put it in a small saucepan or cast-iron casserole with the spices, garlic, and herbs. Pour in enough duck fat to cover the pork by ½ to 1 inch. (If you don't have enough duck fat, add olive oil.) Clip a deep-frying thermometer to the side of the pan and heat over medium heat until the fat registers 200°F on the thermometer. Regulate the heat so the fat maintains this temperature for 20 minutes. Remove the pan from the heat and let cool to room temperature. (The pork can be cooked up to this point, cooled, covered, and refrigerated in its fat for up to 5 days.)

No more than 1 hour before you will sear the pork, make the salad. Peel, halve, and core the apples. Using a mandoline

CURRIED APPLE AND CELERY ROOT SALAD

2 Granny Smith or other tart green apples

2 small or 1 medium celery root

¼ cup cider vinegar

1 tablespoon curry powder

1 teaspoon piment d'Espelette (see page 179)

1 teaspoon kosher salt

3 tablespoons extra virgin olive oil

¼ cup fresh cilantro leaves

1 tablespoon crumbled Garlic Chips (page 178)

Fleur de sel or other coarse salt for finishing

or sharp knife, cut into julienne strips ⅛ inch thick. You should have about 2 cups. Using a paring knife, remove the tough skin from the celery root and cut the flesh into julienne strips. You should have about 2 cups. In a bowl, combine the apples and celery root strips. In a small bowl, whisk together the cider vinegar, curry, piment d'Espelette, salt, and olive oil. Pour about three-fourths of the vinaigrette over the apples and celery root, add the cilantro leaves, and toss until well mixed.

To cook the pork, remove it from the duck fat and wipe off the spices and excess fat with paper towels, leaving a little fat for sautéing. (If the pork has been refrigerated, heat it slowly over low heat just until the fat has liquefied enough for you to remove the meat, and then wipe off the fat and spices.) Cut the pork into ½-inch-thick medallions.

To serve, arrange half of the salad on a platter or plate. Heat a griddle, cast-iron skillet, or sauté pan over medium-high heat until very hot. Add the pork and cook on the first side for 30 seconds, or until golden brown. Using tongs, turn and cook on the second side for 30 seconds, or until golden brown. Place the medallions on top of half of the salad and strew the remaining salad on top of the pork. Drizzle the remaining vinaigrette over all, and sprinkle with the garlic chips and a little fleur de sel.

TO DRINK

Gewürz means "spice" in German, and a Gewüztraminer is usually a reliable match with spicy food. Even though this dish is not spicy in the "hot" sense, it does include a number of assertive spices in the seasoning for the pork and in the curry powder for the salad. A dry, full-bodied Gewürztraminer from a cool growing region in California, such as one from Claiborne & Churchill in the Edna Valley (San Luis Obispo County), is an excellent choice. **B D**

SCALLOPS with LYCHEE GAZPACHO

I am dedicating this dish to my wife, Cameron, who loves scallops, and to one of my longtime and most important employees, busboy Son Ly (I call him the Pillar of Pipérade). Son Ly is Vietnamese, and every summer when the local Asian markets are selling fresh lychees, he brings me far more than I can possibly eat out of hand. I came up with this recipe as a way to use some of the surplus. Because lychees taste best raw, a gazpacho-inspired sauce seemed an ideal way to highlight their flavor. When shopping for lychees, look for fruit that is full and heavy, not shriveled or cracked, and that has a rosy to mottled brown color. They keep well for at least a couple of weeks in the fridge.

The quality and freshness of the scallop can make or break this dish, as with all seafood dishes. Look for "dry-packed" scallops, which means they have not been soaked in a preservative to extend their shelf life. You will also find scallops labeled "day boat" or "diver," indicating that ideally no more than twenty-four hours have passed between the time they were caught and when they were delivered to shore. This is also a good sign of quality, but it is not as critical as dry-packed. Wet-packed scallops will release moisture during cooking and refuse to brown. If you are unsure about the scallops in your fish market, ask the fishmonger.

 Serves 4

½ cup Pedro Ximénez sweet sherry

½ cup sherry vinegar

1 English cucumber

Kosher salt

12 fresh lychees

1 small, ripe tomato, cored and diced

1 tablespoon freshly squeezed lemon juice

¼ cup plus 2 tablespoons extra virgin olive oil

Freshly ground black pepper

8 dry-packed sea scallops (about ¾ pound)

2 tablespoons grape seed oil

1 tablespoon fresh mint leaf chiffonade

¼ cup sliced almonds, toasted

In a small saucepan, bring the sherry and sherry vinegar to a boil over medium-high heat. Reduce the heat to medium-low and cook for about 10 minutes, or until reduced to 2 tablespoons. Set aside.

Peel the cucumber and halve crosswise. Cut half of the cucumber in half lengthwise, remove the seeds, and chop coarsely. Using a mandoline or a sharp knife, julienne the remaining half lengthwise, turning it as you cut so only the outside flesh is used. Discard the seed core. Put the julienned cucumber in a bowl, sprinkle with a little salt, toss to coat, and set aside for 15 minutes while you prepare the sauce and cook the scallops.

To peel a lychee, using a paring knife, cut through the hard outer shell all the way around the fruit down to the seed. Then, using your fingers, peel away the shell and the thin inner skin to reveal the white meat. Pull the meat away from the seed and discard the seed.

CONTINUED

Scallops with Lychee Gazpacho, *continued*

In a blender, combine the lychees, tomato, chopped cucumber, lemon juice, and olive oil and process until smooth. Season the sauce with salt and pepper and set aside. (The sauce can be prepared up to 1 hour ahead, covered, and refrigerated.) It can be served either chilled or at room temperature—whichever you prefer.

Rub the scallops on both sides with the grape seed oil, and sprinkle both sides with salt and pepper. Heat a griddle, cast-iron skillet, or sauté pan over medium-high heat, or until hot. Add the scallops and cook on the first side for 1½ to 2 minutes, or until golden. Using tongs, turn and cook on the second side for 1 to 2 minutes more, or until golden. The scallops should still be slightly translucent in the center (you can make a discreet cut to check). Using the tongs, transfer to a warmed plate.

To serve, divide the lychee sauce evenly among 4 shallow, rimmed bowls or plates. Rinse the julienned cucumber with cold water in a sieve and pat dry with paper towels. Return it to the bowl, toss with the mint, and divide evenly among the bowls, placing a mound in the center. Top each mound with 2 scallops. Strew with the toasted almonds and drizzle with the sherry–sherry vinegar reduction.

TO DRINK

Pour a weighty white to stand up to the scallops, something that has enough fruit to match the lychee and sweet sherry components with enough acid to add balance. A big, unoaked (oak and shellfish are not good together) California Central Coast Chardonnay is just the ticket. Look for a wine from Tolosa (Edna Valley, San Luis Obispo), Mer Soleil (Santa Lucia Highlands, Monterey), or Foxglove (Santa Rita Hills, Santa Barbara). **B F**

SPICED BUTTERFLIED QUAIL ELCANO

Although not as famous as his Portuguese commander, Ferdinand Magellan, navigator Juan Sebastián Elcano was one of many Basque sailors who joined Magellan on his voyage in search of spices in the Moluccas. He became captain of the expedition after Magellan was killed in the Philippines, guiding the diminished expedition back to Spain and completing the first circumnavigation of the globe. The use of the spices in this recipe—cinnamon, cloves, coriander, and cardamom—are my tribute to Elcano.

This recipe calls for boneless quail that have had their backbones and rib cages removed, leaving only the little drumsticks and thighs. You may need to special order them from your butcher and they may come fresh or frozen (which does not affect quality). If you are unsure about cooking them, just remember to do it quickly. Quail are best eaten when the juices run a little pink. **Serves 4**

1 teaspoon coriander seed

3 cardamom pods

1 teaspoon black peppercorns

2 garlic cloves, thinly sliced

1 large shallot, thinly sliced

Grated zest of 1 small orange

¼ teaspoon ground cinnamon

Pinch of ground mace

Pinch of ground cloves

1 tablespoon dark brown sugar

¼ cup extra virgin olive oil

4 boneless quail

Fleur de sel or other coarse salt

Using a mortar and pestle or the bottom edge of a heavy pan, crush the coriander, cardamom seeds (removed from their pods), and peppercorns to a coarse powder. Pour into a small bowl and add the garlic, shallot, orange zest, cinnamon, mace, cloves, brown sugar, and olive oil. Mix well.

If using boneless quail, cut each quail down its back and spread it out so it lies flat. If using bone-in quail, split them along the backbone and press flat. Rub the spice mixture over the entire surface of each quail. Then cover and marinate in the refrigerator for at least 4 hours or up to overnight.

To cook the quail, heat a griddle, cast-iron skillet, or sauté pan over high heat until very hot. Decrease the heat to medium-high, add the quail, skin side down, and cook for about 4 minutes, or until browned. Using tongs, turn and cook on the second side for about 4 minutes, or until browned.

To serve, transfer the birds to a warmed serving platter and sprinkle with the fleur de sel.

TO DRINK

You need a full, fruity red here to stand up to the sweet spices, such as a Pinot Noir from Monterey, California's Miura Vineyards. It has lots of cherry, berry, and plum flavors and a bit of spice to match the marinade seasoning. **B F**

LAMB LOIN with KUMQUAT CHUTNEY

I grew up eating a lot of lamb, which was served not only on special occasions but also for weeknight family meals. I still like to slow cook a shoulder on my days off, but the wonderfully tender Sonoma lamb loins I get for the restaurant are ideal for searing quickly on the griddle and serving with kumquat chutney that can be prepared in advance. Although the ingredients list is long, the chutney is actually easy to prepare and keeps well in the fridge. It is a natural with lamb, of course, but it pairs well with quail, squab, tuna, and swordfish, too. I have even served it as a nontraditional accompaniment to our Thanksgiving turkey.

You can substitute a boneless rack of lamb or even rib or T-bone chops if all you can find are the tiny (1 inch in diameter) lamb loins many retailers sell. Both New Zealand and Colorado lamb are excellent.

 Serves 4 to 6

KUMQUAT CHUTNEY

½ pound kumquats

1 tablespoon olive oil

1½ teaspoons ground coriander

1½ teaspoons ground cumin

1½ teaspoons ground fennel

½ teaspoon ground cardamom

2 tablespoons finely chopped garlic

¼ cup finely chopped shallot

⅓ cup finely chopped fresh ginger

¾ cup golden raisins

¾ cup firmly packed dark brown sugar

3 or 4 points from 1 star anise pod

To make the chutney, quarter the kumquats and try to remove as many seeds as possible using the tip of a paring knife. Bring a saucepan filled with water to a boil, add the kumquats, and boil for 30 seconds. Drain, rinse with cold running water, and set aside. Rinse and dry the saucepan.

Return the saucepan to medium heat and let heat for 30 seconds. Add the oil and all of the ground spices and sauté for 1 to 2 minutes, or until fragrant. Add the garlic, shallot, and ginger and cook, stirring, for 1 to 2 minutes, or until the mixture is dry and crumbly. Add the kumquats, raisins, brown sugar, and star anise, stirring to combine. Add 2 cups water, raise the heat to high, and bring to a boil. Decrease the heat to maintain a simmer and cook, uncovered, for about 1 hour, or until the kumquat rinds are soft and the mixture is thick and syrupy.

Remove from the heat and let cool to room temperature. Transfer to a clean container, cover, and refrigerate for at least 1 day or up to 2 weeks. Bring to room temperature or warm slightly before serving. You should have about 2 cups.

1 pound lamb loin

2 tablespoons olive oil

4 sprigs thyme

2 sprigs rosemary

2 garlic cloves, thinly sliced

Kosher salt and freshly
ground black pepper

Extra virgin olive oil for
drizzling

Coat the lamb with the 2 tablespoons olive oil. Place the lamb, thyme, rosemary, and garlic in a resealable plastic bag. Seal the bag and refrigerate for at least 6 hours or up to overnight.

To cook the lamb, heat a griddle, cast-iron skillet, or sauté pan over medium-high heat until very hot. Remove the lamb from the bag, wiping off and reserving the herbs and garlic. Salt and pepper the lamb generously on all sides. Add to the griddle and cook on the first side for about 2 minutes, or until well browned. Using tongs, turn the lamb to brown on each side for 2 minutes (about 8 minutes total), or until an instant-read thermometer inserted into the thickest part registers 125°F. During the final 2 minutes, put the reserved herb sprigs and garlic slices on top of the lamb. Transfer the lamb with the herbs to a cutting board and let rest for 10 minutes. Discard the garlic.

To serve, cut the lamb into 1½-inch-thick medallions. Arrange the medallions and herbs on a warmed platter. Serve the chutney in a neat mound or small bowl alongside the lamb on the platter.

TO DRINK

The Spanish wine regions of Rioja and Ribera del Duero, both with Denominación de Origen (DO) status, produce medium-bodied, intensely fruity wines that are the traditional match with lamb. Modern-style Riojas, such as those from Finca Allende and San Vicente, with their cherry- and berry-spiced undertones, go nicely with the lamb and the chutney. **M F**

HABAS
shelling beans

BRAISED RED BEANS with MORCILLA

We Basques like our beans. In the past, they nourished us when other forms of protein were scarce. Today, we eat them, both fresh and dried, for their wonderful flavor and texture, and they remain a mainstay of the Basque diet. Particularly prized are the *alubia* (Basque for dried bean) *tolosanas*, from the town of Tolosa, about twenty miles south of San Sebastián. In *pintxos* bars in the region you'll often find *tolosanas* braised with chorizo and served with *guindilla* peppers. Red kidney beans can stand in for the Basque beans, but I encourage you to seek them out from a Spanish food supplier (see Sources). **Serves 6 to 8**

⅓ cup olive oil

½ cup chopped onion

2 tablespoons minced garlic

1 teaspoon fresh thyme leaves

½ teaspoon ground cumin

3 sweet-spiced morcilla sausages, (about ¾ pound) cut into 1-inch-thick slices (see page 182)

1 (15-ounce) can diced tomatoes with juice

2 cups cooked dried red beans (see page 173)

1½ to 2 cups bean cooking liquid, Chicken Stock (page 175), or good-quality commercial chicken stock (see Sources)

Kosher salt and freshly ground black pepper

½ cup fresh cilantro leaves

Heat a large sauté pan over medium-high heat. Add the olive oil and warm the oil until it ripples. Add the onion, garlic, thyme, and cumin and cook, stirring occasionally, for about 3 minutes, or until the onion is translucent and just beginning to color. Add the sausages and cook, stirring occasionally, for 2 to 3 minutes, or until lightly browned. Add the tomatoes and their juice, the beans, and 1½ cups of the bean cooking liquid. Increase the heat to high and bring to a boil. Decrease the heat to maintain a simmer and cook, adding more bean cooking liquid if the beans seem too dry, for 20 minutes, or until the beans are tender. If the beans are too soupy after 20 minutes, increase the heat to high and cook to reduce the liquid. The consistency should fall somewhere between a soup and a stew.

Season to taste with salt and pepper and stir in the cilantro. Transfer to a warmed serving dish and serve.

TO DRINK

It is simple: a deeply flavored rustic stew calls for a full-flavored rustic red from Bierzo. The wines of this rugged, mountainous area of northwestern Spain are made primarily from the Mencéa grape, and have complex aromas of fruit and earth. **B D F**

BLACK-EYED PEA SALAD with CALAMARI

I use beans often in my recipes, but I had never seen black-eyed peas until I came to the United States and a chef friend from the South cooked them for a New Year's party. They are now one of my favorite beans, and I like not only their flavor, but also the little black spots that give them a distinctive look. This is a great dish for at-home dinners because the salad can—and should—be made ahead to allow the flavors to meld. Just before serving, I add a splash of vinegar to brighten the taste.

If the beans have been cooked in advance and refrigerated, warm them up by letting them sit at room temperature for a while or by putting them in the microwave briefly. Room-temperature beans will absorb the flavor of the vinaigrette better. **Serves 4 to 6**

1 pound whole calamari, cleaned (see page 175), or ¾ pound cleaned calamari, tubes cut into ½-inch-wide rings and tentacles left whole

2 cups cooked black-eyed peas (see page 173), at room temperature

1 celery stalk, finely diced

1 ripe tomato, cored and finely diced

3 tablespoons minced shallot

¼ cup fresh tarragon leaves

¼ cup fresh flat-leaf parsley leaves

⅓ cup red wine vinegar

⅓ cup extra virgin olive oil

Kosher salt and freshly ground black pepper

Place a bowl filled with ice water near your stove top. Bring a large saucepan of water to a boil over high heat, drop in the calamari, and cook for exactly 30 seconds. Quickly drain the calamari and plunge them into the ice water. Drain again.

In a large bowl, combine the calamari, beans, celery, tomato, shallot, tarragon, and parsley. In a small bowl, whisk together the vinegar, olive oil, and salt and pepper to taste. Pour the vinaigrette over the calamari and beans mixture and toss until well combined. Taste and adjust the seasoning with salt and pepper. Let the salad sit at room temperature for at least 30 minutes or up to 4 hours before serving to allow the flavors to blend.

TO DRINK

Wines made from Rueda's Verdejo grape are Spain's answer to Sauvignon Blanc. They are fragrantly fruity, with subtle grassy notes and good palate-cleansing acidity, qualities that complement the calamari and will stand up to the tomatoes and vinaigrette. They are also especially good value for their price. **M D**

FAVA BEANS with CRÈME FRAÎCHE and MINT

Every spring when the first crates of fava beans are delivered to the kitchen at Piperade, I can almost hear the collective groan from my kitchen staff all the way from my home twelve miles away. I like favas and use them as often as I can when they are in season, but I have to admit they are labor-intensive, requiring both shelling and peeling. However, from my perspective—and judging from the number of orders we get from our guests—they are worth the work. At home, I hand them to my sons to shell while they watch a baseball game on TV, or I enlist guests before dinner. This recipe is simplicity itself and allows the sweet, nutty flavor of the favas to shine. Try to find small beans; older, larger favas are too starchy to use here. **Serves 4 to 6**

2 pounds fava beans in the pod

½ cup crème fraîche

2 tablespoons extra virgin olive oil

Kosher salt and freshly ground black pepper

⅓ cup mint leaf chiffonade

Finely grated zest of 1 lemon

To prepare the favas, split open the pods and remove the beans. Meanwhile, bring a saucepan filled with salted water to a boil over high heat. Place a bowl filled with ice water near your stove top. Drop the beans into the boiling water and cook for 3 minutes (this is longer than most recipes instruct because the beans are not cooked again). Drain the beans and quickly plunge them into the ice water. With your fingernail, pierce the skin of each bean near one end and squeeze the bean gently to pop free of the skin. Don't worry if the beans separate into halves. You should have about 2 cups beans.

In a bowl, whisk together the crème fraîche, olive oil, and salt and pepper to taste. Add the fava beans, mint leaves, and lemon zest and toss to combine. Cover and refrigerate for at least 30 minutes or up to 2 hours before serving to chill and allow the flavors to meld.

Taste and adjust the seasoning with salt and pepper before serving. Serve chilled.

TO DRINK

The earthy, slightly bittersweet favas and the herbal of the mint call for a zesty, herbaceous Sauvignon Blanc from one of the cooler regions of California. Selene from the Carneros district in Napa Valley meets that description. **M D**

WHITE BEAN and SALT COD STEW
with MARINATED GUINDILLA PEPPERS

When I was growing up, I never had to ask "What's for lunch?" on Fridays. I—and everyone else in the Basque region—could count on salt cod, or *bacalao*. Although the preparations varied, the salted, dried, and rehydrated fish was usually stewed with beans, as in this recipe, or sometimes with potatoes. Despite a childhood filled with *bacalao* meals, I have never grown tired of salt cod, and today I still turn to it when I am stressed or tired, or just want some simple nourishment. Salt cod also provided nourishment for generations of Basque sailors, who, according to Mark Kurlansky in his wonderful book, *Cod*, were fishing the banks off Newfoundland and preserving their catch for the long trip home centuries before Columbus discovered the New World. Today, you can still find a few well-known shops in the Basque Country that sell nothing but salt cod, just as they have for centuries.

This is a classic recipe and according to the way we Basques have always prepared this stew, I ask you to "swirl" rather than "stir" the contents of the casserole. The cod releases gelatin as it cooks and along with the beans creates a creamy emulsion when the pot is gently swirled. **Serves 4 to 6**

¼ **cup olive oil**

½ **cup diced onion**

2 large garlic cloves, thinly sliced

½**-pound piece salt cod, soaked and drained (see page 182)**

2 cups cooked dried cannellini beans or other white beans (see page 173)

1½ cups bean cooking liquid, Chicken Stock (page 175), Veal Stock (page 185), or good-quality commercial chicken or veal stock (see Sources)

Kosher salt and freshly ground black pepper

1 tablespoon aged sherry vinegar

Heat a small casserole or Dutch oven over medium heat. Add the olive oil and warm it until it ripples. Add the onion and garlic and cook, stirring occasionally, for about 4 minutes, or until the onion is translucent but not colored. Lay the cod on top of the onion and cook, turning once, for 5 minutes total. Using a slotted spatula, transfer the cod to a plate.

Add the beans and the bean cooking liquid to the casserole and season with a little salt and pepper. Cover, decrease the heat to maintain a low simmer, and cook for 20 minutes.

Remove about ¾ cup of the beans to a small bowl and mash coarsely with the back of a spoon. Return the beans to the casserole along with the cod. Using the back of the spoon, break up the fish into large pieces. Cook at a low simmer for about 5 minutes longer. Using hot pads, pick up the pan and swirl the contents until they are combined and thickened. Season to taste with salt and pepper and swirl in the sherry vinegar.

GARNISHES

Fried Shallots (page 176)

Garlic Chips (page 178)

4 to 6 whole guindilla peppers packed in vinegar (see page 179), drained

Fresh flat-leaf parsley leaves

Ladle the stew into 4 to 6 shallow, rimmed soup bowls. Garnish each bowl with fried shallots, garlic chips, and a whole pepper. Sprinkle with parsley leaves and serve immediately.

TO DRINK

In recent years, vintners in Galicia have been making a huge effort to plant Godello, a white-wine grape native to the area, because they recognize its potential as a base for high-quality wines. Valdeorras, one of Galicia's five designated growing regions (DOs), is home to the best Godello wines, which are clean, fruity, and rich without being sweet, and have sufficient acidity to make them a great match with this succulent cod stew. **M D**

GIGANTE BEANS with BOQUERONES

From the day we opened Pipérade, this simple, yet sophisticated dish has been on the menu. It is so popular that whenever I take it off, one of our regular customers requests it. I have to admit that the combination of creamy gigante beans, vinegary white anchovies, fresh herbs, and chopped egg is pretty irresistible. Even avowed bean or anchovy haters have been won over by this dish. Gigante beans, which are large Mediterranean white beans, have a unique creamy texture and sweet flavor. They have become the bean darlings of the food world in recent years, and are increasingly available (especially online).

Boquerones (anchovies) cured in vinegar and then packed in oil are common throughout Spain. If you have extremely fresh anchovies, it is a simple process to prepare your own—I think of the two old women outside San Sebastián's La Brecha market filleting the small fish by the bucketful and packaging them in cabbage leaves and newspapers when they make a sale—but even I find it is much easier to buy cured *boquerones* in cans. **Serves 4 to 6**

2 cups cooked dried gigante beans
(see page 173)

4 small piquillo peppers (see page 179), stemmed, seeded, and cut lengthwise into ⅛-inch-wide strips

2 tablespoons minced fresh chives

3 tablespoons chopped fresh flat-leaf parsley

2 tablespoons fresh basil leaf chiffonade

3 tablespoons red wine vinegar

3 tablespoons extra virgin olive oil

Kosher salt and freshly ground black pepper

8 to 12 cured boquerones
(see page 175)

4 to 6 hard-cooked medium eggs, peeled (see page 178)

In a bowl, combine the beans, *piquillo* peppers, chives, parsley, basil, red wine vinegar, and olive oil. Toss well to combine, then season to taste with salt and pepper and toss again. Let sit at room temperature for at least 30 minutes or up to 4 hours before serving to allow the flavors to meld.

To serve, taste and adjust the seasoning with salt and pepper. Mound on a platter or on individual plates. With your hand or the bottom of a glass, lightly smash the eggs to break them open. Place the eggs on top of the beans, arrange 2 *boquerones* on each of the eggs, and serve.

TO DRINK

The Basque region of Irouléguy in the Pyrenees is the westernmost appellation of France. Most of the wines produced there are reds and rosés, but a white Irouléguy, though hard to find, would be perfect with this quintessential Basque combination of *piquillos* and beans. This rare white is full of floral and nutty aromas, and is round but with good acidity. One of my favorite Irouléguys is J. Claude Berrouet's Harry Mina. If an Irouléguy cannot be found, an Albariño, though lighter and more minerally and acidic, would also work. **M D**

POOR MAN'S CASSOULET

The famous *fabadas* of Asturias in Spain and cassoulets of Languedoc and Gascony in France are bean-based winter dishes containing various combinations of preserved meats and sausages. At Fringale, a French bistro that was my first restaurant in San Francisco, the kitchen became known for its cassoulet, but rare is the cook—including myself—who makes it at home, as it requires hard-to-find ingredients and can take days of preparation. One day when playing around in the kitchen, I came up with this simpler version, and while it is nothing compared to a real cassoulet or *fabada*, it is still damn good. The dish makes generous tapas portions, even for six people, and would also work as an entrée for three or four.

Although you can use olive oil in this recipe, I find that duck fat unites the flavors and gives the finished dish a better texture. Many upscale markets and butchers carry it. You can purchase pork belly online or in some ethnic markets. **Serves 6**

⅓ cup rendered duck fat (see Sources) or olive oil

1 piece skinless pork belly (about 1 pound)

½ cup coarsely chopped peeled carrots

½ cup coarsely chopped celery

6 garlic cloves, chopped

1 teaspoon black peppercorns

1 teaspoon dried juniper berries

2 whole cloves

1 large, ripe tomato, cored and cut into ¾-inch cubes

2 tablespoons tomato paste

2 cups dried cannellini beans, picked over, rinsed, soaked, and drained (see page 173)

3 cups Chicken Stock (page 175), Veal Stock (page 185), or good-quality commercial chicken or veal stock (see Sources)

Bouquet garni of 3 or 4 thyme sprigs, 1 bay leaf, and 4 or 5 sprigs flat-leaf parsley, wrapped in a cheesecloth sachet or tied with kitchen twine

In a large casserole or Dutch oven, heat the duck fat over medium-high heat. When the fat is hot, add the pork belly and cook on the first side for 2 to 3 minutes, or golden brown. Using tongs, turn and cook on the second side for about 2 minutes, or until golden brown. Transfer to a plate.

Add the carrots, celery, garlic, peppercorns, juniper berries, and cloves to the pot and cook, stirring occasionally, for about 5 minutes, or until the vegetables have just begun to color. Add the tomato, tomato paste, beans, stock, bouquet garni, and some salt and pepper and stir to dissolve the tomato paste and mix the ingredients well. Return the pork belly to the pot and bring the mixture to a boil. Decrease the heat to maintain a low simmer, cover, and cook for 1½ hours, or until the beans are tender but not falling apart and the pork belly is tender when pierced with a fork.

Remove from the heat. Remove and discard the bouquet garni. Transfer the pork to a cutting board and slice it into pieces ½ inch thick. Stir the pork back into the beans. (At this point, the dish can be cooled, covered, and refrigerated for up to 5 days. Rewarm on the stove top until just warmed through before continuing.)

Kosher salt and freshly ground black pepper

½ to ¾ cup homemade coarse or fine fresh bread crumbs (page 175)

⅓ cup Ham Dust (page 178)

2 tablespoons chopped fresh flat-leaf parsley

To serve, preheat the broiler. Transfer the beans to a shallow, broiler-proof 9 by 13-inch baking dish or divide among 6 shallow baking dishes, each about 5 inches in diameter and 1 inch deep.

Sprinkle the top(s) evenly with the bread crumbs and ham dust. Broil for about 2 minutes, or until the bread crumbs are golden. Garnish with the parsley and serve hot.

TO DRINK

Sometimes when you are not sure whether a rich white or a light red would be better, a serious dry rosé is the perfect choice. That is the case with this dish. Sip a Navarre rosé made from Garnacha grapes. You may enjoy it so much that a siesta will be in order. **L D F**

PIPÉRADE BRAISED BEANS with BAKED EGGS

At its most basic, a *pipérade* is a mixture of sweet peppers, onions, and tomatoes stewed in olive oil. But that description doesn't begin to explain the appeal of this dish, which, for me, is incredibly personal. I grew up on *pipérade*, often eating it at breakfast or midday with eggs, and sometimes for supper with beans and bits of *serrano* ham. It is quintessentially Basque, full of the flavors of the region, and in the nature of all good home cooking, endlessly versatile: a little garlic, a little ham, some beans, making use of whatever is available. I serve this version at home: eggs baked in individual dishes using the *pipérade* and cannellini beans as a base. It can also be prepared in one large (nine by twelve-inch) baking dish. **Serves 6**

3 cups Pipérade (page 181)

2 cups Chicken Stock (page 175), Veal Stock (page 185), or good-quality commercial chicken or veal stock (see Sources)

2 cups dried cannellini beans, picked over, rinsed, soaked, and drained (see page 173)

2-ounce piece smoked ham

2 choricero peppers (see page 179)

6 eggs, preferably farm fresh

Kosher salt and freshly ground black pepper

2 tablespoons fresh flat-leaf parsley leaves

In a large sauté pan, warm the *pipérade* over medium-high heat until hot. Add the stock, beans, ham, and peppers and bring to a boil over high heat. Decrease the heat to maintain a simmer and cook for 1 to 1½ hours, or until the beans are tender all the way through and neither crunchy in the center nor falling apart and mushy. Remove from the heat, and remove and discard the piece of ham and peppers. Let the bean mixture cool for 45 minutes to 1 hour, or until warm or room temperature. (At this point, the dish can be cooled, covered, and refrigerated for up to 5 days. Rewarm on the stove top just until warm before baking with the eggs.) Meanwhile, preheat the oven to 400°F.

Divide the bean mixture among 6 shallow baking dishes, each about 5 inches in diameter and 1 inch deep. Make a small well in the center of the mixture in each dish, and break an egg into each well. Place the baking dishes on a large rimmed baking sheet or directly on the oven rack. Cook for about 15 minutes, or until the egg whites are set but the yolks are still soft.

Remove from the oven and sprinkle each dish with salt and pepper and a few parsley leaves. Serve immediately.

TO DRINK

A superlight, fruity, and young red Garnacha from Navarre, similar in style to Beaujolais, would go well with the smoky ham and sweet peppers. Although eggs are notoriously difficult to match with wine, in this dish they take a backseat to the other flavors and are not a factor in pairing. **L D F**

LENTIL GRATIN with BRAISED SERRANO HAM

Lentils should not be overcooked, particularly if they are going to be used in a salad or in this homey gratin as opposed to a soup where you want them to be soft. They should be separate yet tender and not mushy. Small, green French *lentilles du Puy* hold their shape better than do ordinary brown lentils, and I use them almost exclusively. However, you still must check them often when they are close to being done, as all lentils go from hard to soft quickly. I like to add a drizzle of aged sherry vinegar just before serving to counteract some of the richness and saltiness of the dish. **Serves 6**

⅓ cup olive oil

½ cup chopped peeled carrots

½ cup chopped celery

½ cup chopped onion

2 tablespoons chopped garlic

1 cup lentils, preferably lentilles du Puy, picked over and rinsed (see page 173)

2½ cups Chicken Stock (page 175), Veal Stock (page 185), or good-quality commercial chicken or veal stock (see Sources)

1 end piece or thick slice serrano ham or prosciutto (½ pound) cut into chunks

Bouquet garni of 3 or 4 thyme sprigs, 1 bay leaf, and 4 or 5 sprigs flat-leaf parsley wrapped in a cheesecloth sachet or tied with kitchen twine

Kosher salt and freshly ground black pepper

½ cup to ¾ cup homemade fine fresh bread crumbs (page 175)

Aged sherry vinegar for drizzling

Heat a large casserole or Dutch oven over medium-high heat. Add the olive oil and warm it until it ripples. Add the carrots, celery, onion, and garlic and cook, stirring occasionally, for about 5 minutes, or until the vegetables have just begun to color. Add the lentils and stir for 1 minute. Add the stock, ham, and bouquet garni and bring to a boil. Decrease the heat to maintain a low simmer and cook for 30 to 45 minutes, or until the lentils are tender but not falling apart. Start testing the lentils after 30 minutes, testing them every few minutes.

Remove from the heat. Remove and discard the bouquet garni. Remove the ham to a cutting board, let it cool slightly, and finely chop it. Stir the chopped ham back into the lentils, and season to taste with salt and pepper. (At this point, the dish can be cooled, covered, and refrigerated for up to 3 days. Rewarm on the stove before continuing.)

To serve, preheat the broiler. Transfer the lentils to a shallow, broiler-proof 9 by 13-inch oval baking dish or divide among 6 shallow baking dishes, each about 5 inches in diameter and 1 inch deep. Sprinkle the top(s) evenly with the bread crumbs, using ½ cup if using a single dish and ¾ cup if using individual dishes. Broil for about 2 minutes, or just until the bread crumbs are golden brown. Drizzle with vinegar and serve.

TO DRINK

Imagine the warm fall sun of Andalusia casting its warmth on you while you sip some pale, dry, refreshing fino sherry from a *copita* (small glass) and eat this rustic dish. Life doesn't get better. **M D**

WHITE BEAN SALAD with MANCHEGO, AVOCADO, APPLE, and MEYER LEMON

I usually make this pretty little salad in the fall, when the last of summer's basil is at the farmers' market and Meyer lemons and local apples are starting to appear. Meyer lemons are a common presence in California yards and gardens. They're sweeter and less acidic than the average supermarket Eureka lemon, which is why you'll need less juice in the recipe if you use regular lemons. ✺ **Serves 4 to 6**

1 large avocado, halved, pitted, peeled, and cut into ½-inch dice

1 large Granny Smith or other tart green apple, peeled, halved, cored, and cut into ½-inch dice

1½ cups cooked small white beans (see page 173)

3 ounces Manchego cheese, cut into ¼-inch dice (about ½ cup)

¼ cup fresh basil leaf chiffonade

¼ cup pine nuts, toasted

⅓ cup freshly squeezed Meyer lemon juice or ¼ cup regular lemon juice

¼ cup extra virgin olive oil

Kosher salt and freshly ground black pepper

In a bowl, combine the avocado, apple, beans, cheese, basil, and pine nuts and toss gently to mix. Whisk together the lemon juice and olive oil in another small bowl and toss gently with the bean mixture until combined. Season to taste with salt and pepper. The salad should not be mixed more than 30 minutes before serving so the apple and avocado don't darken.

TO DRINK

Overlooked Pinot Blanc wines from California often offer more value and complement food better than the state's much-heralded Chardonnays. Here, they are creamy enough to match the avocado, generally pair well with cheese, and have enough zip to stand up to the vinaigrette. Monterey County's Chalone Vineyard makes particularly fine Pinot Blancs. **L F D**

BOCADILLOS
little sandwiches

WATERCRESS with "PERFECT BLONDE" WALNUTS and ROASTED PEACHES

The family of my friend Chris Madsen owns a Chandler English walnut orchard in California's Central Valley, and in early fall he always brings me a huge bag of what he calls his "perfect blondes," the nuts that receive the top grade for their pale color and sweet flesh. (I like using the term on my menu just to hear my customers ask, "What's a perfect blonde?") Happily, in California, the beginning of the season for walnuts coincides with the end of the peak season for locally grown watercress and stone fruits. Instead of serving this dish as a salad—not that it wouldn't be good that way—I decided to put everything into a bread roll and serve it as a small sandwich. Perfect! **Makes 4 sandwiches**

1 tablespoon olive oil

1 or 2 firm but ripe peaches or nectarines, pitted and sliced ½ inch thick (4 to 8 slices total)

1 teaspoon sugar (optional)

4 small French dinner rolls, split horizontally

1½ cups loosely packed watercress leaves

½ cup chopped walnuts

1½-ounce piece Manchego cheese, very thinly sliced or shaved with a vegetable peeler

Freshly ground black pepper

Heat a medium sauté pan over high heat until hot. Add the olive oil and warm it until it ripples. Add the peach slices and cook for 1 minute, or until they begin to brown slightly but are still firm. Turn and cook on the second side for 1 minute longer, or until beginning to brown. If the fruit is not very sweet, sprinkle the slices with the sugar before browning to nudge them toward caramelizing. Transfer to a plate.

To serve, lightly toast the cut sides of the rolls. Top the bottom of each roll with one-fourth of the watercress leaves, 1 or 2 warm peach slices, and one-fourth each of the walnuts and Manchego. Grind pepper on top, and close the rolls. Put a skewer through each sandwich to hold it together.

TO DRINK

Viognier wine, with its floral aroma, lush tropical-fruit flavors, and dry finish will nicely complement the sweet peaches, slightly bitter walnuts, and peppery watercress. Plantings of Vigonier are limited in its native France, but California's Joseph Phelps began experimenting with the grape in the 1980s, and today a number of excellent West Coast labels are available. **M F**

ROASTED EGGPLANT SPREAD
with BOQUERONES

This is an unpretentious *bocadillo*, made of humble ingredients: eggplant roasted with garlic, rustic whole-wheat bread, and marinated anchovies. It can be topped with cheese or roasted tomatoes, though I prefer the simple contrast of creamy eggplant and vinegary *boquerones* (marinated white anchovies). I only make this *bocadillo* in late summer when eggplant is at its peak of flavor, sweet and not bitter. To slice the bread thinly, partially freeze the loaf and cut it with an electric knife or on a meat slicer. **Makes 8 open-faced sandwiches**

1 large globe eggplant (about 1¼ pounds)

Kosher salt

2 tablespoons extra virgin olive oil

½ teaspoon ground cumin

1 large garlic clove, thinly sliced

Freshly ground black pepper

2 tablespoons chopped fresh cilantro

8 slices whole-wheat batard or other rustic whole-wheat French bread, ¼ inch thick

8 cured boquerones (see page 175)

Trim off the stem end of the eggplant, and cut the eggplant in half lengthwise. Sprinkle the flesh with salt. Turn flesh side down in a colander, and let sit in the sink or over a bowl for 30 minutes to drain. Preheat the oven to 400°F.

Wipe off the salt on the eggplant halves. Score the cut side of each half in a 1-inch crosshatch pattern, cutting about ½ inch deep. Rub evenly with the olive oil and cumin, and insert the garlic slices into the cuts. Sprinkle with a little more salt and some pepper. Place the halves, cut side up, on a rimmed baking sheet and roast for about 1 hour, or until browned and completely soft.

Remove from the oven, let cool slightly, and scoop the flesh into a bowl, discarding the skin. Mash with a fork and season with salt and pepper. Stir in the cilantro. (At this point, the eggplant can be covered and kept at room temperature for up to 4 hours or refrigerated for up to 2 days. If refrigerated, bring to room temperature before continuing.)

To serve, lightly toast the bread slices. Spread the slices with the eggplant, and top each with 1 *boquerón*.

TO DRINK

The wine options are limited here because there are only two flavor factors to consider: the intense spices in the eggplant and the vinegary *boquerones*. A crisp, dry, powerful manzanilla sherry is the best choice. **L D**

FIGS MARINATED in SHERRY
with AGED GOAT CHEESE and BASIL

Every year in late summer, I wait for the season's first Black Missions and Kadotas to arrive at the market. When I was a kid, I used to watch the figs ripen on our neighbor's tree so I could steal them the moment they reached perfection (I think she knew but never told my parents). Now I use the luscious fruits in many dishes, usually in supporting roles. This simple little *bocadillo*–sherry-marinated fig slices paired with aged goat cheese on toasted bread–is my favorite way of letting the fresh flavor of figs dominate. Monte Enebro, an excellent salty, tangy, aged Spanish goat cheese from an artisanal producer in Avila, is the best choice, but Humboldt Fog, an aged goat cheese from Cypress Grove, California, sold throughout the United States, is an excellent stand-in. **Makes 4 open-faced sandwiches**

4 ripe but firm Black Mission or Kadota figs

1 teaspoon sherry vinegar

1 teaspoon Pedro Ximénez sweet sherry

Freshly ground black pepper

4 slices rustic whole-wheat bread, ¾ inch thick

2 to 4 ounces aged goat cheese (see headnote), softened at room temperature

1 tablespoon fresh basil leaf chiffonade

Cut off the stem from each fig, and slice the figs lengthwise ¼ inch thick. Lay the slices in a single layer on a plate. In a small bowl, stir together the sherry vinegar and sherry, and brush or spoon onto the figs. Sprinkle with pepper. Let marinate at room temperature for 1 hour.

To serve, lightly toast the bread. Spread one side of each slice generously with the goat cheese. Divide the fig slices evenly among the bread slices, arranging them on top of the goat cheese. Sprinkle with the basil.

TO DRINK

This pairing requires a leap of faith. Imagine a small—but not too small—glass of golden sweet Jurançon from the French Basque region that is full of fruit but not cloying and has a racy acidity and exceptional body, such as the one produced by Clos Uroulat. You will be pleasantly surprised. **B F**

CHOPPED EGG SALAD
with CAPER BERRIES and FRESH HERBS

This recipe, like most of the *bocadillos* in this chapter, calls for only a few ingredients, which makes it imperative that you use the best you can find and prepare them with care. Fresh herbs are a must and how you prepare the hard-cooked eggs is critical. I ask you to refer to the pantry for my preferred method, which produces creamy yellow yolks and non-rubbery whites. Caper berries, the pickled, small, marble-size fruit of a common Mediterranean bush called *Capparis spinosa* (the more familiar nonpareil capers are buds of the same plant), are imported in jars from Spain. They're milder and less salty than small capers but still should be rinsed before use. **Makes 4 open-faced sandwiches**

4 hard-cooked eggs (see page 178), peeled

2 sprigs chervil

2 sprigs tarragon

2 sprigs flat-leaf parsley

2 fresh basil leaves

3 tablespoons extra virgin olive oil

Kosher salt

4 slices pain de mie, about ¾ inch thick, or other French white sandwich bread, crusts removed

½ teaspoon piment d'Espelette (see page 179)

12 caper berries, rinsed and dried

Roughly chop the eggs and put them in a bowl. Roughly chop the chervil, tarragon, parsley, and basil and add to the eggs along with the olive oil. Stir to combine, season to taste with salt, and stir again.

To serve, lightly toast the bread slices and spread with the egg salad. Sprinkle evenly with the *piment d'Espelette* and top each sandwich with 3 caper berries.

TO DRINK

This dish has wine-pairing characteristics similar to those for White Bean and Salt Cod Stew with Marinated Guindilla Peppers (page 36). You have creamy, rich eggs combined with tangy caper berries, so you need a wine that is not fruity and has good acid. Again, Godello is the choice here. **M D**

WARM TOASTED BREAD
with TOMATO SPREAD and SERRANO HAM

Almost nothing is more satisfying in late summer than a sandwich of sliced garden-fresh tomatoes, a little coarse salt, and maybe some mayonnaise on artisanal bread. The traditional rustic Catalan way of serving this dish calls for rubbing the cut half of a ripe tomato on grilled bread, but I like my presentation a little more refined. I turn very ripe tomatoes into a puree and serve it alongside grilled bread and sliced *serrano* ham. It makes a perfect starter for a casual outdoor meal, sort of an assemble-it-yourself affair. The recipe is flexible. Amounts can be increased depending on the number of guests, and everything can be served on a platter—the bowl of tomato puree, a stack of bread, the ham slices—family style. **Serves 4 to 6**

TOMATO PUREE

1½ pounds ripe tomatoes
(4 to 5 medium-large)

1 small garlic clove, minced

1 tablespoon extra virgin olive oil

Kosher salt and freshly ground
black pepper

4 to 6 slices crusty French bread,
sweet or sourdough

4 to 6 thin slices serrano ham

Extra virgin olive oil for drizzling

To make the tomato puree, bring a large saucepan filled with water to a boil. Have a bowl filled with ice water near your stove top. With a small knife, cut out the stem of each tomato and score the blossom end with an X. Immerse the tomatoes in the boiling water for 15 to 30 seconds, or until the skins start to loosen. Scoop out with a slotted spoon and plunge into the ice water to stop the cooking. Peel the tomatoes, halve them through their equators, and gently squeeze to remove the juice and seeds. Roughly chop the tomato pulp.

In a food processor, combine the tomato pulp, garlic, and olive oil and process until finely chopped. Season to taste with salt and pepper. Transfer to a serving bowl, cover, and set aside at room temperature for up to 4 hours.

To serve, toast or grill the bread slices. Stack them on a serving platter alongside the bowl of tomato puree and the ham slices. Invite guests to spread the toast with the puree and top with a slice of ham. Pass the olive oil for drizzling on top.

TO DRINK

When choosing a wine for this dish, how the dish is served is as much of a consideration as the flavors in the food. The tomatoes, garlic, and olive oil all call for something rich and acidic, but the casualness of the presentation brings a tapas bar to mind. A fino sherry is a worthy complement. **M D**

GRIDDLED HAM and CHEESE BOCADILLOS

The beauty of this dish lies in the simplicity of its ingredients, and while they must be top-notch—ripe toma-toes, artisanal sheep's milk cheese, and authentic *serrano* ham or prosciutto—what you use to cook the sandwiches can be either low-tech or high-tech. If you have a fancy panini grill, either stove top or electric, use it, following the manufacturer's directions. If not, a stove-top griddle or grill pan and a cast-iron skillet to press the sandwiches will work just as well. 🌀 **Makes 4 sandwiches**

8 slices sourdough French bread, ½ inch thick

8 thin slices serrano ham or prosciutto

8 slices ripe tomato, ¼ inch thick

4 thin slices sheep's milk cheese such as P'tit Basque, Manchego, or Ossau-Iraty

Dijon mustard for spreading

2 tablespoons extra virgin olive oil

Lay 4 bread slices on a work surface. Top each slice with a slice of ham, 2 tomato slices, a slice of cheese, and another slice of ham. Spread the remaining bread slices on one side with mustard, and place, mustard side down, on top. Tuck in any over-hanging portions of the filling so they won't burn.

Brush the outsides of the bread with the olive oil. Preheat a stove-top griddle or ridged grill pan over medium-high heat. Place the sandwiches on the hot surface, top with a weight, and grill, turning once, for about 2 minutes on each side, or until both sides are golden brown and the cheese is softened.

To serve, cut the sandwiches in half.

TO DRINK

Put tomatoes, strong mustard, and salty cheese between bread slices (which, when you come down to it, is just a grilled cheese sandwich) and you need something not too serious to wash it down. A fresh, fruity, sprightly red Rioja *joven* (young), served slightly chilled, is a good match. **L D F**

MR. WILLIAMS'S FRIED CHICKEN SANDWICH

People who have not met him might be surprised to learn that Chuck Williams, founder of legendary kitchenware chain Williams-Sonoma, has very simple tastes. At ninety-three, he is an inspiration to me for many reasons, not the least of which is that he still goes into the office every day. He frequently orders this fried chicken sandwich at the café we operate at the Williams-Sonoma corporate headquarters. In fact, he has ordered it so often we felt compelled to name the sandwich for him. ❧ **Makes 2 or 4 sandwiches to serve 4**

1 skinless, boneless chicken breast half (about ½ pound)

½ cup all-purpose flour

1 egg, beaten

1 cup panko (Japanese bread crumbs)

Kosher salt and freshly ground black pepper

Olive oil for frying

2 good-quality hamburger buns or Kaiser rolls

¼ cup Aioli (page 172) or mayonnaise

½ ripe avocado, peeled and thinly sliced

1½-ounce piece Manchego cheese

2 piquillo peppers (see page 179), stemmed, seeded, and each cut into 2 pieces

4 large fresh basil leaves

½ cup arugula leaves, tossed with a little extra virgin olive oil

Halve the breast crosswise. One at a time, place the halves between sheets of parchment paper or plastic wrap and pound them until they are an even ⅓ to ½ inch thick. Line up 3 shallow, wide bowls on a work surface. Set a wire rack over a rimmed baking sheet and set the baking sheet nearby. Put the flour in the first bowl, the beaten egg in the second, and the panko in the third. Season both sides of each chicken piece with salt and pepper. One at a time, dip the chicken pieces first in the flour, shaking off the excess, then in the egg, and finally in the panko, patting both sides to make sure the chicken is evenly coated and crumbs are adhered. Place the breaded chicken pieces on the rack and set aside. (The chicken can be prepared to this point and refrigerated for up to 4 hours.)

Just before serving, cook the chicken. Pour olive oil to a depth of ¼ inch into a skillet and heat over medium-high until the oil shimmers but doesn't smoke. Add the chicken and fry for 2 minutes, or until golden brown. Using tongs, turn and cook on the second side for 2 minutes, or until golden. Using the tongs, transfer the chicken to paper towels to drain.

To serve, if necessary, split the buns or rolls in half horizontally. Spread the cut sides with a thin layer of aioli. Divide the avocado slices evenly between the bottoms. Using a cheese planer or vegetable peeler, shave the cheese into thin slices, and place the slices on the avocado. If using rolls, cut each chicken piece in half. Place a warm chicken piece, 2 *piquillo* pepper pieces (or 1 piece if using rolls), 2 basil leaves (or 1 leaf if using rolls), and an equal amount of the arugula on each bun or roll half. Close the buns or rolls. If using buns, cut the sandwiches in half, and skewer each half with a toothpick to keep it together. If using rolls, leave whole and skewer with a toothpick to keep it together.

TO DRINK

Rather than contrasting the richness of the fried chicken, avocado, aioli, and cheese with an acidic wine, highlight it with a lush, soft, full mouthfeel, dry wine, such as a white Priorat (made primarily from the Garnacha grape). **B D**

SEARED TUNA with ONION MARMALADE

Not long ago, I ate one of these sandwiches for lunch, probably because there was not much else left in the kitchen at Bocadillos that day. I was stunned at how delicious it was. My surprise came not because of the ingredients—I have always liked the combination of fresh tuna and onion marmalade—but rather because this sandwich has been on all of my menus since I opened my first restaurant. Frankly, it had become boring to me, so I had stopped eating it. That spur-of-the-moment lunch reminded me of just how good this sandwich is.

The onion marmalade makes about one and a half cups, and you will only need about one-quarter cup for the sandwiches. The remainder can be stored in the refrigerator for up to a week and used in other sandwiches or served alongside roasted meats. **Makes 4 sandwiches**

ONION MARMALADE

2 large onions, thinly sliced

2 cups balsamic vinegar

2 cups sherry vinegar

1 ahi (yellowfin) tuna fillet, ½ pound and at least 1-inch thick

Kosher salt and freshly ground black pepper

1 tablespoon olive oil

4 small French dinner rolls, split horizontally

¼ cup Aioli (page 172) or mayonnaise

1 small roasted red bell pepper (see page 179), cut lengthwise into ½-inch-wide strips

2 cups mixed salad greens

Extra virgin olive oil for drizzling

To make the onion marmalade, in a large saucepan, combine the onions, balsamic and sherry vinegars, and 2 cups water and bring to a boil over high heat. Decrease the heat to maintain a low simmer and cook uncovered, stirring occasionally, for 1½ to 2 hours, or until the onions have softened completely and the liquid is syrupy. If the mixture begins to dry out before the onions are ready, add a little more water. If it is too watery, increase the heat to cook off the excess moisture. Remove from the heat and let cool to room temperature. The marmalade will keep at room temperature for up to 4 hours or in the refrigerator for up to 1 week.

Heat a sauté pan over high heat until very hot. Meanwhile, sprinkle the tuna liberally on all sides with salt and pepper. When the pan is hot, add the oil and let it heat for a few seconds. Add the tuna and cook on the first side for 1 to 1½ minutes, or until lightly browned. Using tongs, turn and cook on the second side for 1 to 1½ minutes, or until lightly browned. The outer ¼ inch of each side should be cooked and the interior should be rare. Transfer to a cutting board and let sit for a few minutes while you prepare the sandwiches.

Spread the bottom cut sides of each roll with about
1 tablespoon aioli and about 1 tablespoon onion marmalade.
Slice the tuna about ¼ inch thick, and divide the slices evenly
among the bottoms of the rolls. Top with the pepper strips,
dividing them evenly. Place the greens in a small bowl, drizzle
with a little extra virgin olive oil, sprinkle with salt and pepper,
and toss to mix. Place one-fourth of the dressed greens in a
small mound on top of the pepper strips. Close the rolls.

TO DRINK

Jam (fruity) plus roasted pepper (earthy) plus tuna (red but not
too meaty) equals Pinot Noir. There are many terrific Pinots
from California, with some of the best from Sonoma's Russian
River Valley and the Central Coast counties of Monterey and
San Luis Obispo. **L D F**

CUMIN-SCENTED LAMB BURGERS

These aromatic ground lamb "sliders" have been on the menu at Bocadillos since day one and are now something of a signature dish. Bob Petzold, the talented chef there, wanted to create a lamb burger but realized it would be too rich and intense to serve in a normal hamburger-size portion. These meatball-size burgers, stuffed into rich buns, were the perfect solution. ✿ **Makes 4 small burgers**

1 tablespoon cumin seed

2 tablespoons Aioli (page 172) or mayonnaise

½ teaspoon coriander seed

½ teaspoon fennel seed

1 pound ground lamb

4 small brioche, challah, or other small, soft buns, split horizontally

2 tablespoons olive oil

1 shallot, thinly sliced

4 small, thin slices ripe tomato

4 small butter lettuce leaves, from center of head

In a spice grinder, grind the cumin seed to a fine powder. Transfer ½ teaspoon ground cumin to a small bowl, add the aioli, mix well, and set aside. Pour the remaining ground cumin into a second small bowl. Combine the coriander and fennel seeds in the spice grinder and grind to a fine powder. Add to the ground cumin and mix well.

In a bowl, combine the lamb and mixed ground spices and knead lightly until well combined. Divide the lamb mixture into 4 equal portions. Form each portion into a patty a little wider than the buns and set aside (you want them wider because they shrink when you cook them). Or the patties can be covered and refrigerated for up to 8 hours before continuing.

To serve, lightly toast the cut sides of the buns. Heat a large sauté pan over medium-high heat. Add the oil and warm it until it ripples. Add the lamb patties and cook on the first side for about 3 minutes, or until browned. Using a spatula, turn and cook for 3 to 4 minutes, or until browned on the second side but still lightly pink in the center. Transfer to paper towels.

Spread the cut sides of each bun with the cumin aioli. Divide the shallot slices evenly among the bun bottoms. Top with a burger, a tomato slice, a lettuce leaf, and a bun.

TO DRINK

Wines made from either one of two Spanish varietals, Garnacha and Tempranillo, would go well with this casual dish of meaty ground lamb with spices. That typically means buying a wine from Spain's Rioja or Ribera del Duero region. But you can also opt for an earthy, spicy, dry wine such as Cecilia Tejada's Tempranillo from California, a blend of Tempranillo and Garnacha. **M D F**

ESTOFADOS
stews and braises

OCTOPUS MURCIA

One of my all-time favorite food memories happened on a trip to Spain with two good friends, chef Laurent Manrique and wine guru Jorge Ordoñez. After a night of great camaraderie and heavy indulgence, we found ourselves in a small restaurant in the town of Murcia, in southeast Spain, seeking a morning-after restorative lunch. We sat looking at a bubbling fire-fueled caldron filled with beer and an enormous—possibly as big as twenty-five pounds—octopus. As our mouths dropped open, the cook retrieved the creature from the brew, cut the tentacles into small pieces, and topped them with a sprinkle of coarse sea salt and a drizzle of fruity olive oil. None too delicately we pounced on the octopus pieces, which were meaty and tender and a little yeasty from the beer, and then washed everything down with more of the local quaff. I don't know whether it was the octopus or the beer, but all was right with the world for me for the rest of the day.

Look for cleaned, uncooked whole octopus in Asian and Latin markets. We use San Francisco–made Anchor Steam beer at Bocadillos, but any good-quality beer will work. **Serves 4**

1 cleaned whole octopus (about 4 pounds)

1 carrot, cut into 1½-inch pieces

1 onion, cut into 1½-inch pieces

1 celery stalk, cut into 1½-inch pieces

½ head garlic

2 tablespoons black peppercorns

3 to 6 (12-ounce) bottles beer, depending on the size of the pot

1 tablespoon chopped shallot

3 tablespoons freshly squeezed lemon juice

⅓ cup extra virgin olive oil

½ cup fresh cilantro leaves

Kosher salt and freshly ground black pepper

½ pound fingerling or small Yukon gold potatoes, cooked, cooled, and cut into lengthwise wedges

Fleur de sel or other coarse salt for finishing

Put the octopus into a large casserole or Dutch oven and add the carrot, onion, celery, garlic, peppercorns, and enough beer to come halfway up the sides of the pot. Bring to a boil over high heat, cover, and decrease the heat to maintain a simmer. Cook for 45 minutes, uncover, and continue to simmer for another 45 minutes, or until the octopus is tender when pierced with a fork. The octopus will swell up and look like it is going to come out of the pan. But don't worry because it will shrink back down. Remove the octopus from the pan, and discard the cooking liquid.

In a small bowl, whisk together the shallot, lemon juice, olive oil, and cilantro leaves to make a vinaigrette. Season to taste with salt and pepper and set aside.

To serve, using kitchen scissors, cut the tentacles from the octopus body, and discard the head and body. Then make cuts 1 inch apart the length of each tentacle, being carefully not to cut all all the way through. In a bowl, combine the tentacles and potatoes, add the vinaigrette, and toss to coat evenly.

CONTINUED

Octopus Murcia,
continued

Serve each person an equal amount of the potatoes and 2 tentacles. Sprinkle with sea salt.

TO DRINK

Just as with the black-eyed pea salad on page 33, a medium-bodied, fruity, very crisp Rueda made from Verdejo grapes is called for here. **M D**

CLAMS with SPICY SMOKED TOMATOES

One afternoon, I watched the guys in the kitchen scorch a pile of tomatoes over the gas flame of the stove to make salsa for the staff meal. Nearby was another pile of tomatoes we were about to use in a sauce for clams. Seeing that second pile made me wonder why we didn't roast those tomatoes, too. We did, and the clam dish was the hit of that evening's dinner menu. Now we always smoke the tomatoes for this simple dish of steamed clams. You can use a specially designed stove-top smoker (which can be purchased online or in kitchen-supply stores), or you can throw some soaked wood chips on a still smoldering barbecue after dinner, put the tomatoes on the grill rack, and leave them for about twenty minutes. Smoked tomatoes will keep in the refrigerator for up to three days. ❧ **Serves 4 to 6**

1¼ pounds ripe tomatoes, cored, halved, and smoked (see headnote)

¼ cup olive oil

1 small onion, finely diced

3 garlic cloves, minced

2 teaspoons red pepper flakes

1 cup dry white wine

Kosher salt and freshly ground black pepper

3 pounds Manila clams, scrubbed

½ cup flat-leaf parsley sprigs

Fruity extra virgin olive oil for drizzling

Peel the smoked tomatoes and cut into ½-inch dice. You should have about 2 cups.

Heat a large sauté pan over medium-high heat until hot. Add the olive oil and warm it until it ripples. Add the onion, garlic, and red pepper flakes and cook, stirring occasionally, for 3 to 4 minutes, or until the onion is translucent and just beginning to color. Add the wine, bring to a boil over high heat, and cook for 5 minutes, or until the liquid is reduced by half. Add the smoked tomatoes and a few generous pinches of salt. Stir to combine and return the liquid to a boil. Add the clams, cover, and cook, stirring every couple of minutes, for 6 to 8 minutes, or until the clams begin to open. Remove from the heat and check the sauce for seasoning, adding more salt and some pepper if necessary.

To serve, remove and discard any clams that failed to open. Transfer the clams to a warmed rimmed platter, scatter the parsley over the top, and drizzle with extra virgin olive oil. For a casual family-style presentation, you can serve the clams directly from the sauté pan. The clams are also good served at room temperature.

CONTINUED

Clams with Spicy
Smoked Tomatoes,
continued

TO DRINK
Albariño, Spain's star-studded white variety, has found an
interesting home in several wineries in California. Havens,
in the Carneros district in Napa, was one of the first producers to try its hand at it and has succeeded admirably. The
California wines are richer and more powerful than their
more delicate Spanish counterparts, but they complement this
full-flavored stew because they are minerally enough to pair
with the clams and have enough acid to cut the intensity of
the smoked tomatoes. **L D**

SPICY and SWEET CHICKEN WINGS

Both of my restaurants, Piperade and Bocadillos, are on the edge of San Francisco's Chinatown, and sometimes when I have a taste for something different than my own food, I will head to one of the nearby Chinese restaurants. Inspired by the Asian flavors of ginger, garlic, pungent fish sauce, and chiles, I created this recipe for sautéed chicken wings, which has become a favorite staff meal served with rice. The Chinese wisely know that the middle joint of the chicken wing (picture the section between the wing tip and "drumstick") has the most flavor because of its ratio of meat to bone. Certainly feel free to use the meatier "drumsticks" if that's what you prefer. **Serves 4 to 6**

2 tablespoons minced fresh ginger

2 tablespoons minced garlic

Grated zest and juice of 1 lemon

½ cup soy sauce

1 tablespoon Vietnamese fish sauce (nuoc mam)

2 tablespoons Sriracha chile sauce

¼ cup honey

2 pounds (about 24) chicken wings, middle joint only, or chicken "drumsticks"

2 tablespoons grape seed or canola oil

In a bowl, whisk together the ginger, garlic, lemon zest and juice, soy sauce, *nuoc mam*, chile sauce, and honey until well combined. Add the chicken wings and toss to coat well. Let marinate at room temperature for 30 minutes or in the refrigerator for up to 2 hours.

Heat a large sauté pan over medium heat until hot. Add the grape seed oil and warm it until it ripples. Add the chicken wings and cook, stirring occasionally, for 20 minutes, or until golden and the liquid is beginning to thicken. Increase the heat to medium-high and reduce the liquid for about 5 minutes, or until it has glazed the wings.

Remove from the heat and serve the wings hot or at room temperature.

TO DRINK

With the hot, sweet, tart, and salty food of Asia, fruity, light, crisp, well-balanced sweet wines, such as Riesling and Gewürztraminer, are classic options. A California Riesling produced by Ventana Vineyards in Monterey's Salinas Valley is both delicious and reasonably priced. **L F**

MONKFISH IN OLIVE OIL, TOMATO, and SAFFRON

Monkfish, also called anglerfish, is popular throughout the Mediterranean, and is often called poor man's lobster because its dense, sweet flesh also tastes vaguely of the shellfish, the diet of the angler. It is widely available in U.S. fish markets throughout the year, and I like to prepare it most often in the summer when ripe tomatoes and fresh basil are at their peak. A cook's warning: Don't be tempted to add more saffron than specified in the recipe. The flavor of saffron gets bigger as it cooks and infuses the liquid. **Serves 4**

1 pound monkfish fillet

½ cup olive oil

1½ cups diced onion

2 tablespoons chopped garlic

¼ teaspoon loosely packed saffron threads

2 large, ripe tomatoes, preferably heirloom, cored and cut into large cubes

⅓ cup pitted green olives, quartered lengthwise

¼ cup capers, rinsed and drained

Kosher salt

⅓ cup loosely packed fresh basil leaves, coarsely chopped

If your fishmonger has not removed the membrane from the monkfish, use needle-nosed pliers to peel it away, and then cut the fish into 4 equal pieces. Set the pieces aside.

Heat a casserole or saucepan over medium-high heat until hot. Add the olive oil and warm it until it ripples. Add the onion, garlic, and saffron and cook, stirring occasionally, for 3 to 4 minutes, or until the onion is translucent and just beginning to color. Stir in the tomatoes, cook for a few seconds, and then cover and decrease the heat to low. Cook for 20 minutes to blend the flavors.

Uncover, add the olives and capers, and increase the heat if necessary to bring the liquid to a bare simmer. Sprinkle the monkfish pieces on both sides with a little salt and put them on top of the tomato sauce. Cover and cook over low heat for 5 minutes, or until the monkfish is opaque. Sprinkle in the basil, recover, and remove from the heat. Let rest for 5 minutes before serving.

TO DRINK

The luxurious texture and flavor of the monkfish combined with the complexity of the spices calls for a luscious, full-bodied white with some structure. A respectable white Rioja, such as one from Marqués de Murrieta or Allende, will do the job. **M D**

CHICKEN THIGHS with SPICY BASQUE "KETCHUP"

It is the addictive sauce that makes this dish special. Sweet from the peppers and brown sugar, spicy from the *piment d'Espelette*, and tangy from the vinegar, the sauce is easy to put together, can be made in quantity (this recipe makes three-quarter cup but can be increased easily three or four times), and is good with everything from these chicken thighs to eggs and fried potatoes. **Serves 4**

4 skin-on chicken thighs

Kosher salt and freshly ground black pepper

2 tablespoons olive oil

2 tablespoons dark brown sugar

¼ cup sherry vinegar

1 heaping cup Pipérade (page 181), pureed

2 teaspoons piment d'Espelette (see page 179)

Chopped fresh flat-leaf parsley for garnish

Preheat the broiler.

Sprinkle the chicken on all sides with salt and pepper. Heat a sauté pan over high heat until hot. Add the olive oil and warm it until it ripples. Add the chicken, skin side down, and cook for 3 to 4 minutes, or until the skin is golden brown. Using tongs, turn and cook on the second side for 3 minutes, or until lightly browned. Transfer the chicken to a plate and discard the oil.

Return the pan to high heat and add the brown sugar, whisking until it melts. Remove from the heat and whisk in the sherry vinegar. Return the pan to medium heat and whisk the mixture for about 1 minute, or until it has thickened and reduced. Stir in the *pipérade* and the *piment d'Espelette*. Return the chicken to the pan, cover, decrease the heat to low, and cook for 10 minutes, or until the thighs are cooked through.

Transfer the chicken, skin side up, to a broiler pan and broil for about 2 minutes, or until the skin is crisp.

To serve, spoon a pool of the sauce on each warmed plate and top with a chicken thigh. Sprinkle with the parsley.

TO DRINK

The Navarre region is in north-central Spain, and its food is strongly influenced by the Basque Country, which borders it. Most of the grapes grown there are Garnacha, and though it was long thought of as the region of *rosadas*, or rosés, its reds are gaining in popularity. A spry, light, fruity Navarre red, served slightly chilled, is ideal here. **L D F**

SPICY LAMB MEATBALLS
with CUCUMBER SALAD

Endlessly versatile, meatballs of one kind or another have been on our menu at Bocadillos since we opened. We have used various meats and flavor combinations, but these lamb meatballs, redolent with garlic, cumin, and coriander and spicy from red pepper flakes, have become one of our most popular tapas. At home, I double the recipe so that I can put some in the freezer to have on hand for an impromptu hors d'oeuvre party. I recommend that you grind your own spices for the freshest flavor, but for the sake of convenience, you can double or triple the amount and keep the ground mixture in a tightly closed container in the pantry for a month or so.

To keep the meatballs light, mix the ingredients with your hands, rather than a spoon, until it is just barely combined. ✾ **Makes 16 meatballs; serves 4**

MEATBALLS

1 tablespoon olive oil

1 shallot, minced

2 small garlic cloves, minced

1 tablespoon red pepper flakes

2 tablespoons cumin seed

1 tablespoon coriander seed

1 tablespoon fennel seed

¾ pound ground lamb

2 eggs

½ cup homemade coarse fresh bread crumbs (page 175)

2 teaspoons kosher salt

To make the meatballs, heat a large sauté pan over medium-high heat until hot. Add the olive oil and warm it until it ripples. Add the shallot, garlic, and red pepper flakes and cook, stirring occasionally, for about 1 minute, or until the shallot and garlic are softened but not browned. Transfer to a bowl and let cool. Set the pan aside to use for cooking the meatballs.

In a spice grinder, grind the cumin, coriander, and fennel seeds to a fine powder.

Add the lamb to the shallot mixture along with the ground spices, eggs, bread crumbs, and salt. Using your hands, lightly mix together all of the ingredients just until combined. Using about 2 tablespoons of the meat mixture for each meatball, form into 16 golf ball–size balls and set aside on a plate. (The meatballs can be shaped, covered, and refrigerated for up to 8 hours or frozen for up to 2 months and thawed in the refrigerator before use.)

To make the cucumber salad, put the cucumber slices in a colander or sieve and toss with the salt. Let sit for 10 minutes and then squeeze lightly to remove the liquid and drain well. Put the drained cucumbers in a bowl, add the vinegar reduction, olive oil, lemon zest, and mint leaves, and stir gently to mix.

CUCUMBER SALAD

1 English cucumber, peeled and very thinly sliced, preferably on a mandoline

2 tablespoons kosher salt

3 tablespoons Moscatel vinegar reduction (see page 178)

1 tablespoon extra virgin olive oil

¼ teaspoon grated lemon zest

¼ cup loosely packed fresh mint leaf chiffonade

3 tablespoons grape seed or canola oil

Red pepper flakes or piment d'Espelette (see page 179), optional

To serve, return the sauté pan to medium-high heat and heat until hot. Add the grape seed oil and warm it until it ripples. Add the meatballs, being careful not to crowd them in the pan. (Or cook them in 2 batches.) Cook, turning with tongs every few minutes, for about 10 minutes, or until browned evenly on all sides. The meatballs should be just barely cooked through and even a little pink. Transfer the meatballs to a plate to rest for 5 minutes before serving.

Divide the cucumber salad among 4 small plates, arranging the salad in a small mound on each plate. Top with the meatballs, dividing them evenly. Garnish with a sprinkle of red pepper flakes if you enjoy heat.

TO DRINK

Wines made from Tempranillo grapes are versatile food wines—they taste good with everything—and a dry, fruity rosé made from a classic Rioja Tempranillo is the perfect complement to the spiced lamb and cucumber salad. Look for Viña Ijalba Aloque or Marqués de Cáceres. **L D F**

BRAISED LAMB SHOULDER with FIDEO PASTA in PARMESAN CRUST

Throughout Spain, you will find braised meat or seafood dishes made with a fine pasta called *fideo* that resembles short pieces of vermicelli. In towns along the Spanish Mediterranean, cooks prepare *fideuá*, a kind of seafood paella that uses *fideo* instead of rice. This lamb dish, which sautés the same pasta until golden and cooks it in stock before combining it with the meat, is similar to one I ate growing up. To create a textural contrast, I cover the top with bread crumbs and toast it under a broiler. A satisfying peasant dish, it can be served in small portions with other tapas, or as a main course with a green salad.

Fideo pasta can be found at stores that sell Spanish food products and in upscale food markets. You can substitute vermicelli (though not capellini, which is too thin) broken into half-inch pieces.

 Serves 4 to 6

2 tablespoons olive oil

1½-pound piece boneless lamb shoulder

1 onion, chopped

1 carrot, chopped

1 celery stalk, chopped

3 or 4 garlic cloves, left whole

2 large, ripe tomatoes, cored and cut into chunks

1 cup dry white wine

Bouquet garni of 5 or 6 sprigs thyme, 1 bay leaf, and 6 to 8 sprigs flat-leaf parsley wrapped in a cheesecloth sachet or tied with kitchen twine

2 tablespoons kosher salt

1 tablespoon black peppercorns

1 cup Veal Stock (page 185), Chicken Stock (page 175), or good-quality commercial chicken or veal stock (see Sources), or as needed to almost cover

Preheat the oven to 350°F.

Select a small casserole or Dutch oven in which the lamb will fit snugly and heat over high heat until hot. Add the olive oil and warm it until it ripples. Add the lamb and cook on the first side for about 3 minutes, or until browned. Turn the lamb and cook on the second side for about 3 minutes, or until browned. Transfer to a plate.

Add the onion, carrot, celery, and garlic to the casserole over high heat and cook, stirring, for about 3 minutes, or until lightly browned. Return the meat to the casserole, add the tomatoes and the wine, and bring to a boil. Cook for about 6 minutes, or until the liquid is reduced by half. Add the bouquet garni, salt, peppercorns, and enough stock almost to cover the meat. Cover and place in the oven for about 1 hour, or until the meat is tender when pierced with a fork.

Transfer the meat to a cutting board. Strain the liquid through a fine-mesh sieve into a large glass measuring cup. You should have about 2 cups. Let sit for about 20 minutes, or until the fat rises to the surface. Skim off the fat and discard it. (You can also refrigerate the liquid so the fat congeals on the surface, making it easier to remove.) Coarsely chop the lamb and set it aside. Reserve the braising liquid for cooking the *fideo*.

FIDEO

2 tablespoons extra virgin olive oil

3 tablespoons finely chopped onion

2 garlic cloves, chopped

1 cup (about 4 ounces) fideo pasta (see headnote)

Reserved lamb braising liquid

¼ cup homemade coarse fresh bread crumbs (page 175)

¼ cup freshly grated Parmesan cheese

To make the *fideo*, in a flameproof baking or gratin dish large enough to hold the finished dish or in a medium sauté pan, heat the oil over medium heat until it ripples. Add the onion and garlic and cook, stirring occasionally, for 5 minutes, or until translucent and softened. Stir in the pasta and cook, stirring, for 1 minute, or until it begins to turn opaque. Add 1 cup of the lamb braising liquid, decrease the heat to medium-low, and cook at a low simmer, stirring occasionally to prevent sticking and adding a little more braising liquid as the liquid reduces, for about 20 minutes, or until the pasta is tender and the liquid is almost completely absorbed.

Stir in the chopped lamb and cook for a minute or so to heat the mixture thoroughly. If you used a sauté pan, transfer the mixture to a baking dish that can be put under the broiler. (The dish can be prepared up to this point, cooled, and refrigerated for up to 1 day, and then covered and reheated in a 350°F oven for about 30 minutes, or until warmed throughout, before continuing.)

To serve, preheat the broiler. In a small bowl, stir together the bread crumbs and Parmesan cheese. Spread the crumb mixture evenly over the lamb and pasta mixture. Broil until the crust is golden brown. Let sit for a few minutes before serving.

TO DRINK

Meat stews with many layers of flavor call for bold, rustic reds to mirror them. An old-vine Priorat, such as those made from Garnacha and Cariñena grapes, will warm you just as the dish will. An exemplary example is the Miserere from Costers del Siurana, one of Spain's greatest wineries. **B D F**

OXTAILS BRAISED in RED WINE

Europeans and Asians generally recognize how delicious and succulent this bony beef cut is, but I have found that oxtails are a hard sell for many Americans. It occurred to me that they may be too darn much work to eat for relatively little meat, so I decided to come up with a recipe that featured oxtails in a more user-friendly form. This is a great way to serve oxtails to squeamish or bone-adverse eaters, though it is not easy on the cook. The oxtails are braised and then the meat is picked from the bones and formed into sausage-like logs. Although the process is labor-intensive, it is not at all difficult, and all of the work can be done in advance of serving, making this a perfect dish for entertaining.

The tart parsley salad cuts the richness of the oxtails. You can also serve this dish as main course for four, accompanied with boiled potatoes or glazed pearl onions. 🌀 **Serves 6 to 8**

¼ **cup olive oil**

2 **pounds oxtails, cut crosswise into 2-inch pieces**

Coarse sea salt and freshly ground black pepper

1 **onion, chopped**

1 **carrot, chopped**

1 **celery stalk, chopped**

1 **(750-ml) bottle dry red wine**

Bouquet garni of 1 bay leaf, 6 sprigs thyme, and 6 to 8 sprigs flat-leaf parsley wrapped in a cheesecloth sachet or tied with kitchen twine

½ **head garlic**

2-**inch piece fresh ginger**

2 **tablespoons black peppercorns**

2 **cups Veal Stock (page 185), Chicken Stock (page 175), or good-quality commercial chicken or veal stock (see Sources), or as needed to almost cover**

¾ **cup homemade fine dry bread crumbs (page 175), seasoned with kosher salt and freshly ground black pepper**

2 **tablespoons olive or grape seed oil**

Preheat the oven to 350°F.

Heat a medium casserole or Dutch oven over high heat until hot. Add the ¼ cup oil and warm it until it ripples. Sprinkle the oxtails with salt and pepper, add to the casserole, and cook for about 8 minutes, turning to brown them on all sides. Transfer to a plate.

Decrease the heat to medium-high, add the onion, carrot, and celery, and cook, stirring, for 2 to 3 minutes, or until lightly browned. Return the meat to the casserole and add the wine, bouquet garni, garlic, ginger, and peppercorns. Increase the heat to high, bring to a boil, and cook for about 6 minutes, or until the liquid is reduced by half. Add the stock and some salt, and return to a boil. Cover and place in the oven for about 2 hours, or until the meat is fork-tender.

Transfer the cooked oxtails to a plate. Strain the liquid through a fine-mesh sieve into a large glass measuring cup to cool. You should have about 4 cups. Let sit for about 20 minutes, or until the fat rises to the surface. (You can also refrigerate the liquid so the fat congeals on the surface, making it easier to remove.) Skim off the fat and discard it. Pour the defatted liquid into a saucepan, place over high heat, bring to a boil, and cook for about 12 minutes, or until reduced to 1 cup. Remove from the heat and let cool for 10 minutes.

PARSLEY SALAD

2 cups loosely packed
flat-leaf parsley

2 teaspoons red wine or
sherry vinegar

1 tablespoon extra virgin olive oil

Coarse sea salt and freshly ground
black pepper

Using your fingers (gloves help protect from the heat), remove the meat from the bones, and discard the bones along with any fat and gristle. You should have about 3 cups (1 pound) meat. Season to taste with salt and pepper. Cover and refrigerate both the meat and the reduced sauce for at least 2 hours or up to 2 days.

To form the oxtail meat into a log, place a piece of plastic wrap about 18 inches long by 11½ inches wide on a work surface, with the long edge parallel to the edge of the counter. (Sprinkle the underside with a little water to help keep it in place.) Place the oxtail meat on the plastic wrap, positioning it near the center but closer to the counter edge, and shape it into a 10-inch-long log. Lift the edge of the plastic wrap nearest you up over the meat and tuck it in a little around the log. Using a straightedge such as a ruler or the blunt edge of a chef's knife, press in against the plastic, fitting it tightly against the meat and shaping the meat into an even log. The log should be about 12 inches long and 2½ inches in diameter. Simultaneously twist the ends of the plastic wrap in opposite directions to compress the log into a tight roll. Tie each twisted end with kitchen twine to secure, and refrigerate the oxtail log for at least 4 hours or up to 2 days.

To serve, preheat the oven to 450°F.

Leaving the plastic wrap on, and using a sharp slicing or chef's knife, cut the log into 6 to 8 rounds each about 1½ inches thick. Carefully remove the plastic wrap from each round, and press the bread crumbs onto 1 cut side of each round. Heat a large, ovenproof nonstick skillet or sauté pan over high heat until hot. Add the 2 tablespoons olive oil and warm it until it ripples. Add the oxtail rounds, crumb side down, and cook for about 1 minute, or until browned. Using tongs or a spatula, carefully turn the rounds crumb side up and transfer the pan to the oven (if the pan doesn't fit in the oven, transfer the rounds

CONTINUED

Oxtails Braised in Red Wine, *continued*

to a rimmed baking sheet). Bake for about 8 minutes, or until the rounds are heated through.

While the rounds are in the oven, reheat the sauce. To make the parsley salad, place the parsley leaves in a bowl, drizzle with the vinegar and olive oil, and toss to coat evenly. Season with salt and pepper.

To serve, place each hot oxtail round on an individual plate, and arrange a small mound of the salad alongside. Drizzle a little sauce over each round and sprinkle with coarse salt.

TO DRINK

The relatively small Castilian wine region of Toro, which is often overshadowed by its bigger neighbors, Rueda and Ribero del Duera, is known for heady red wines made primarily from Tempranillo grapes. Those from Dehesa Gago are medium bodied and full of fruit and have soft tannins that insist on being acknowledged but won't overwhelm your palate. They marry well with the filling, flavorful oxtails. **B D F**

BEEF SHORT RIBS in MOSCATEL

I like beef short ribs and have cooked them in what seems like a million ways: braised, stewed, and grilled, with nearly every spice and flavor imaginable. But I keep coming back to this simple recipe. It has a hint of Asian spice; the subtle sweetness of Moscatel wine, a Spanish dessert wine; and the tartness of Moscatel vinegar, all of which complement the rich beef. A late-harvest Sauvignon Blanc from California can be used instead of Moscatel. ✤ **Serves 4 to 6**

2 pounds flanken-style beef short ribs, about 2½ inches thick

Kosher salt and freshly ground black pepper

¼ cup olive oil

1 onion, chopped

1 carrot, chopped

1 celery stalk, chopped

1 (750-ml) bottle Moscatel wine

Bouquet garni of 5 or 6 sprigs thyme, 1 bay leaf, and 6 to 8 sprigs flat-leaf parsley wrapped in a cheesecloth sachet or tied with kitchen twine

½ head garlic

½ jalapeño chile, stemmed and halved lengthwise

1 teaspoon coriander seed

1 teaspoon Sichuan peppercorns

½ teaspoon fennel seed

1 cinnamon stick

3 star anise pods

3 whole cloves

2 cups Veal Stock (page 185), Chicken Stock (page 175), or good-quality commercial chicken or veal stock (see Sources), or as needed to almost cover

2 tablespoons Moscatel vinegar

Chopped fresh flat-leaf parsley for garnish

Preheat the oven to 350°F.

Cut the ribs between the bones so you have individual pieces. Sprinkle them on both sides with salt and pepper. Heat a large casserole or Dutch oven over high heat until hot. Add the olive oil and warm it until it ripples. Add the ribs to the casserole and cook for about 8 minutes, turning to brown them on all sides. Transfer to a plate.

Decrease the heat to medium-high, add the onion, carrot, and celery, and cook, stirring, for 2 to 3 minutes, or until lightly browned. Return the ribs to the casserole and add the wine, bouquet garni, garlic, chile, and all of the spices. Increase the heat to high, bring to a boil, and cook for about 6 minutes, or until the liquid is reduced by half. Add the stock, season with salt, and bring to a boil. Cover and place in the oven for about 1 hour, or until the meat is fork-tender.

Transfer the ribs to a plate. Leave the oven on. Strain the liquid through a fine-mesh sieve into a large glass measuring cup to cool. You should have about 4 cups. Let sit for about 20 minutes, or until the fat rises to the surface. (You can also refrigerate the liquid so the fat congeals on the surface, making it easier to remove.) Skim off the fat and discard it. Pour the defatted liquid into a saucepan, place over high heat, bring to a boil, and cook for about 12 minutes, or until reduced to 1 cup. Remove from the heat and add the vinegar. (The ribs can be returned to the liquid, cooled, covered, and refrigerated for up to 2 days before continuing. The flavor of the dish will improve during this rest period.)

To serve, reheat the ribs in the sauce in the oven until warmed through. Taste the sauce and add another splash of vinegar and some salt and pepper if needed. Arrange the ribs on a warmed rimmed platter and pour the sauce over the top. Garnish with the parsley.

TO DRINK

A red made from Garnacha grapes with spice, acidity, and body is a natural match with this Asian-spiced version of short ribs. A Montsant, especially the one from Arrels, is an excellent choice. (Full disclosure is in order here: this is a wine I produce in partnership with friends Laurent Manrique, Emmanuel Kemji, and Sylvain Portay.) **M D F**

ORGANOS
innards

LAMB'S TONGUE with MÂCHE
and PIQUILLO PEPPERS

Every time I pass the Basque Hotel in San Francisco's North Beach, not far from my restaurants, I think about the large number of immigrants who settled throughout California and the West after the gold rush, and how hotels and boardinghouses were at the center of their lives. Hotels were places to celebrate weddings, birthdays, and baptisms, and boardinghouses offered food, lodging, and familiar community to newly arrived (and often lonely) men seeking their fortunes. This is the kind of dish I imagine being served family style at one of those boardinghouses.

Basque cooks know how to use offal and consider it a waste, if not a sacrilege, to throw away any part of an animal. Lamb's tongue is considered a delicacy, and when prepared properly—simmered leisurely until tender, skinned, and trimmed of all bones, fat, and gristle before slicing—it is a delicious addition to salads with a vinaigrette that contrasts with the succulent meat. (See photo page 87.) **Serves 4 to 6**

1¼ pounds lamb's tongues (about 6)

1 carrot, cut crosswise into 3 pieces

1 onion, quartered lengthwise

1 celery stalk, cut crosswise into 3 pieces

5 garlic cloves, left whole

Bouquet garni of 5 or 6 sprigs thyme, 1 bay leaf, and 6 to 8 sprigs flat-leaf parsley wrapped in a cheesecloth sachet or tied with kitchen twine

1 tablespoon black peppercorns

VINAIGRETTE

3 tablespoons sherry vinegar

1 large shallot, julienned lengthwise

1 tablespoon fresh mint leaf chiffonade

3 tablespoons extra virgin olive oil

Kosher salt and freshly ground black pepper

In a large saucepan, combine the tongues, carrot, onion, celery, garlic, bouquet garni, peppercorns, and water to cover the tongues by 2 inches. Bring to a boil over medium-high heat, decrease the heat to maintain a simmer, and cook uncovered (adding more water if necessary) for 1½ hours, or until the tongues are tender when pierced with a fork but still offer a little resistance.

Transfer the tongues to a plate and let cool just until you can handle them. Peel off the skin and trim away any fat, small bones, and gristle from the underside (base) of the tongues. If cooking the tongues in advance, strain the broth through a fine-mesh sieve, return the peeled tongues to the broth, cover, and refrigerate for up to 2 days. Reheat the tongues gently until warm in the broth before serving, or remove from the broth and bring the tongues to room temperature.

(The broth can be discarded if you're not using it to store the tongues.)

To make the vinaigrette, in a small bowl, whisk together the vinegar, shallot, mint, olive oil, and salt and pepper to taste.

4 cups mâche leaves

3 piquillo peppers (see page 179), stemmed, seeded, and cut lengthwise into ⅛-inch-wide strips

Fleur de sel or other coarse sea salt for finishing

To serve, cut the warm or room-temperature tongues crosswise into ¾-inch-thick slices and place on each of 4 plates. Top with mounds of mâche and the *piquillo* peppers, dividing them evenly. Drizzle with the vinaigrette, and sprinkle with the sea salt.

TO DRINK

Many American wine drinkers still think of rosés as sweet and cheap, but nothing could be further from the truth. Travel throughout Spain and France and you will find serious, complex, bone-dry versions made from a variety of grapes. A Rioja rosé is a sound match for this dish. **L D F**

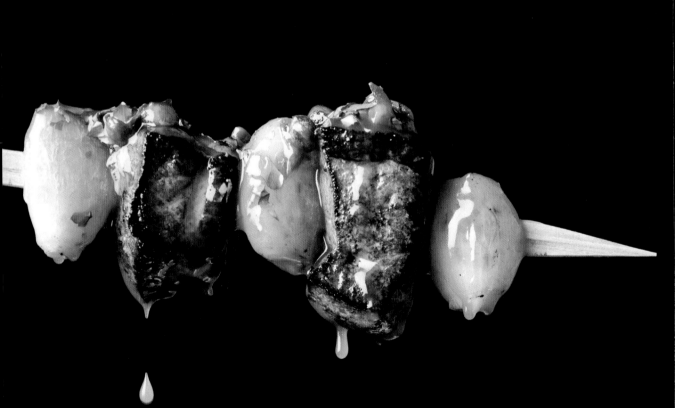

CALF'S LIVER and CARAMELIZED
SHALLOT BROCHETTES

I grew up with a mother, who like all good nurturing mothers everywhere, encouraged her children to eat liver because it was good for them. She didn't have to work too hard to convince me because I have always liked organ meats, particularly calf's liver, which when properly cooked is tender and subtly flavored. Onions are a classic accompaniment, but in an unusual presentation, I thread lightly sautéed cubes of liver and whole caramelized shallots onto skewers and serve them drizzled with a tart-salty pan sauce of capers and lemon juice. ❧ **Serves 4**

CARAMELIZED SHALLOTS

8 small to medium shallots

1 generous tablespoon unsalted butter

1 teaspoon sugar

1 teaspoon kosher salt

¾ pound calf's liver

Kosher salt and freshly ground black pepper

2 tablespoons olive oil

2 tablespoons capers, rinsed and drained

Juice of 1 lemon

1 tablespoon extra virgin olive oil

1 tablespoon chopped fresh flat-leaf parsley

To make the shallots, in a small skillet, combine the shallots, butter, sugar, salt, and 2 cups water and bring to a boil over high heat. Decrease the heat a little and cook at a vigorous simmer, uncovered, for 12 to 15 minutes, or until the shallots are tender when pierced with a knife and the water has evaporated. As the shallots cook, use tongs to turn them a few times so they cook evenly, adding more water if necessary to prevent sticking before the shallots are ready. When they are done, they should be tender throughout, golden, and glazed. Transfer the shallots to a plate and set the skillet aside while you prepare the liver. (The shallots can be cooked up to 8 hours ahead and kept at room temperature.)

Trim away any skin and membrane from the liver, and cut into 8 equal cubes. Pat the cubes dry with paper towels and sprinkle with salt and a generous amount of pepper.

Place a paper towel–lined plate near the stove top. Heat the same skillet over medium-high heat until hot. Add the olive oil and warm it until it ripples. Arrange the liver cubes in the pan in a single layer without touching. (If they do not fit comfortably, cook them in 2 batches.) Cook, turning once with tongs, for 1 to 2 minutes on each side. (How long you cook them depends on the thickness of the pieces and the doneness you prefer. I like them pink-red in the center.)

CONTINUED

Calf's Liver and
Caramelized Shallot
Brochettes, *continued*

Transfer to the towel-lined plate to drain. Turn off the heat but leave the skillet on the burner. Immediately add the capers, lemon juice, extra virgin olive oil, and parsley to the pan and swirl the pan or stir the contents to combine the ingredients into a sauce.

To serve, have ready 4 small bamboo skewers. Alternately thread 2 liver cubes and 2 shallots onto each skewer. Arrange the skewers on a platter and pour the sauce over the top.

TO DRINK

Sherry is probably the most undervalued of the great classic wines, and few wine types have as much variety in a single category. Calf's liver, which can be amazingly sweet and at the same time beefy and unctuous, pairs well with a nutty and raisiny, yet dry amontillado. **B D**

MORCILLA in CIDER

The Basques have had a centuries-old love affair with hard apple cider (called *sidra* or *sagardoa*), and even today they continue to visit cider houses in the winter for barrel tastings. Fans of both hard cider and *morcilla*, Spain's popular blood sausage, will appreciate their marriage in this dish in which the cider—and fresh apples—highlight the inherent sweet spiciness of the sausage. It is a good addition to a tapas spread, or can be served as a main course for a modest lunch, with just crusty bread for sopping up the juices and maybe a tart arugula salad. See the Pantry (page 182) for a fuller description of the blood sausage.

 Serves 4 to 6

2 tablespoons olive oil

1 small onion, thinly sliced

2 garlic cloves, thinly sliced

3 sweet-spiced morcilla sausages (about ¾ pound total) sliced ½ inch thick (see page 182)

2 Granny Smith or other tart green apples, peeled, halved, cored, and cut into ½-inch cubes

1½ cups hard cider

1 teaspoon piment d'Espelette (see page 179)

Fresh flat-leaf parsley leaves for garnish

Heat a large sauté pan over medium-high heat until hot. Add the olive oil and warm it until it ripples. Add the onion and garlic and cook, stirring occasionally, for about 5 minutes, or until the onion is softened and lightly browned. Add the sausage slices and continue to cook, stirring a few times, for about 2 minutes, or until the slices have begun to brown slightly. Add the apples and cider and bring to a boil. Stir, cover, and cook, still over medium-high heat, for 2 to 3 minutes, or until the apples are still somewhat firm. Uncover, stir, and cook for 3 to 4 minutes longer, or until the liquid reduces a bit.

To serve, using a slotted spoon, transfer the sausages and apples to a warmed rimmed platter or plate. Reduce the liquid over high heat until thickened slightly, stir in the *piment d'Espelette*, and pour over the sausages and apples. Sprinkle with the parsley.

TO DRINK

Here, the cooking liquid is also the best choice for the table, pairing well with the sweetness of the apples and the intensely flavored sausage. Pour a traditional Basque hard cider, such as Bereziartua, available online (see Sources). **L F**

CRISPED PIG'S TROTTERS
with EGG and FRESH HERB SALAD

Even people who confess their love for pork seem to shy away from pig's feet, or trotters. That surprises me because some of the best meat on the hog is found on the foot. Trotters do, however, require quite a bit of work on the part of the cook, which is probably the reason more avid pork eaters don't prepare them. Although this recipe requires commitment in terms of time and effort, none of the steps is difficult and all of them must be done in advance, making it a great dish for entertaining. The trickiest task is to form the boned meat into a log, though it sounds more difficult than it is. It is easiest to pick the meat from the feet while they are still warm, so wear gloves to protect your hands from the heat. Then you need to "mush up" the skin and meat to release their natural gelatin, which will help hold the chilled log together. The log is sliced and finished with a coating of bread crumbs, and served with a salad to create a textural and acidic contrast to the rich meat.

For a surefire method for hard-cooked eggs, see page 178. ❋ **Serves 6**

2½ pounds pig's trotters (about 3)

1 carrot, cut crosswise into 3 pieces

1 celery stalk, cut crosswise into 3 pieces

1 small onion, studded with 3 whole cloves

1½ teaspoons black peppercorns

1½ teaspoons dried juniper berries

Bouquet garni of 5 or 6 sprigs thyme, 1 bay leaf, and 6 to 8 sprigs flat-leaf parsley wrapped in a cheesecloth sachet or tied with kitchen twine

4 teaspoons kosher salt

2 tablespoons distilled white vinegar

1 small shallot, minced

2 tablespoons Dijon mustard

2 teaspoons sherry vinegar

Freshly ground black pepper

In a large saucepan, combine the pig's trotters, carrot, celery, onion, peppercorns, juniper berries, bouquet garni, 2 teaspoons of the salt, white vinegar, and water to cover the trotters by 2 inches. Bring to a boil, decrease the heat to maintain a gentle simmer, cover, and cook for 3 hours, or until the trotters are very tender when pierced with a fork.

Transfer the trotters to a bowl and let cool just until you can handle them. Discard the broth or strain and reserve for another use. Using your fingers (gloves help protect from the heat), remove the bones from the trotters, keeping the meat and skin intact as much as possible. Still using your hand, crush the meat and skin into small pieces. Add the shallot, mustard, sherry vinegar, remaining 2 teaspoons salt, and pepper to taste and mix well.

To form the trotter meat into a log, place a piece of plastic wrap about 18 inches long by 11½ inches wide on a work surface, with the long edge parallel to the edge of the counter. (Sprinkle the underside with a little water to help keep it in place.) Place the trotter meat on the plastic wrap, positioning it near the center but closer to the counter edge, and shape it into a

EGG SALAD

4 hard-cooked eggs (see page 178), peeled and coarsely chopped (about ½-inch pieces)

1 small shallot, minced

1 tablespoon Dijon mustard

1 tablespoon sherry vinegar

2 tablespoons extra virgin olive oil

Leaves from 1 or 2 sprigs each tarragon, chervil, flat-leaf parsley, and chives, or whatever is on hand, finely chopped

Kosher salt and freshly ground black pepper

½ cup Dijon mustard

1 cup homemade fine fresh bread crumbs (page 175)

1 tablespoon olive oil

2 cups mixed salad greens

Aged balsamic vinegar for drizzling

Fruity extra-virgin olive oil for drizzling

10-inch-long log. Lift the edge of the plastic wrap nearest you up over the meat and tuck it in a little around the log. Using a straightedge such as a ruler or the blunt edge of a chef's knife, press in against the plastic, fitting it tightly against the meat and shaping the meat into an even log. The log should be about 9 inches long by 3 inches in diameter. Simultaneously twist the ends of the plastic wrap in opposite directions to compress the log into a tight roll. Tie each twisted end with kitchen twine to secure, and refrigerate the trotter roll for at least overnight or up to 2 days.

To make the egg salad, in a bowl, stir together the eggs, shallot, mustard, sherry vinegar, olive oil, and herbs until combined. Season to taste with salt and pepper. Refrigerate in a covered container until serving or up to 1 day ahead.

To serve, preheat the oven to 500°F.

Leaving the plastic on, and using a sharp slicing or chef's knife, cut the log into 6 equal rounds each about 1½ inches thick. Carefully remove the plastic wrap from each round, and spread both cut sides of each round with a little of the mustard. Press the bread crumbs on both sides of each round, dividing them evenly. Heat a large nonstick skillet or sauté pan over high heat until hot. Add the olive oil and warm it until it ripples. Add the trotter rounds, cut side down, and cook for about 1 minute, or until browned. Using tongs or a spatula, carefully turn the rounds over and transfer the pan to the oven (if the pan doesn't fit in the oven, transfer the rounds to a rimmed baking sheet). Bake the rounds for about 5 minutes, or until heated through.

CONTINUED

Crisped Pig's Trotters
with Egg and Fresh Herb
Salad, *continued*

To serve, place each hot trotter round on an individual plate, and arrange a small mound of the egg salad alongside. Place the greens in a bowl, drizzle with a little balsamic vinegar and extra virgin olive oil, and toss to coat evenly. Serve the greens alongside the trotter rounds and egg salad, and then lightly drizzle the rounds with balsamic vinegar and extra virgin olive oil.

TO DRINK

This dish is loaded with strong flavors and unctuous textures, and you need a wine that will cut through and balance them. A light, fruity, and well-structured young (joven) Rioja, served slightly chilled, is an excellent companion. **L D F**

TRIPE AITA

My mother and father were both good cooks, and both of them had definite opinions about how things should be done in the kitchen. But this dish was my father's—his alone—so my mother never said a word about it. I like to call it the "tripe of my father," *aita* being the Basque word for "father." It is a rustic family-style dish that satisfies the appetite and nourishes the soul.

As you cook honeycomb tripe, it will throw off a lot of liquid, which eliminates the need for stock and flavors the sauce. Like most braises, this tastes even better the next day. ✥ **Serves 4**

2 tablespoons olive or grape seed oil

1 large onion, sliced ¼ inch thick or thinner

½ cup garlic cloves, chopped

2 red bell peppers, cored, seeded, and cut lengthwise into ½-inch-wide strips

1½ pounds honeycomb beef tripe, purchased partially cooked, cut into 1-inch squares

1 large, ripe tomato, cored and coarsely chopped

1 tablespoon tomato paste

Bouquet garni of 5 or 6 sprigs thyme, 1 bay leaf, and 6 to 8 sprigs flat-leaf parsley wrapped in a cheesecloth sachet or tied with kitchen twine

Kosher salt and freshly ground black pepper

¼ cup homemade coarse fresh bread crumbs (page 175)

Heat a large saucepan over medium-high heat. Add the oil and warm it until it ripples. Add the onion, garlic, and bell peppers, stir, reduce the heat to medium, and cook, stirring occasionally, for 10 to 15 minutes, or until the vegetables have softened and begun to turn golden. Stir in the tripe, tomato, and tomato paste and add the bouquet garni and enough water to just barely cover. Bring to a boil over high heat, decrease the heat to maintain a simmer, and cook uncovered for 1 hour, or until the tripe is tender when pierced with a fork (or try biting into a piece).

Remove from the heat. If the tripe and vegetables have given off a lot of liquid and the sauce seems thin, strain the contents of the pan and set the tripe and vegetables aside. Return the liquid to the pan, bring to a boil, and cook until reduced to 1½ cups. Stir the tripe and vegetables into the reduced sauce and season with salt and pepper. Decrease the heat to medium to reheat the tripe and thicken the sauce further. The dish should be stewlike, neither soupy nor dry. (At this point, the dish can be cooled, covered, and refrigerated for up to 3 days. Reheat before continuing.)

To serve, preheat the broiler. Transfer the tripe, vegetables, and sauce to a broiler-proof shallow gratin dish or 4 individual baking dishes. Scatter the bread crumbs evenly on top, and broil until golden.

TO DRINK

This dish calls for something not too heavy or too fruity. A dry Tempranillo from Penedès, in Catalonia, is perfect. **M D**

OXTAIL EMPANADAS with SPICY MANGO DIP

This recipe is time-consuming, but the results are worth the effort. When I serve these empanadas at parties, they always disappear. The recipe can be doubled or even tripled and made in stages, over several days, and then the pastries can be frozen. Sometimes I even dig a couple of empanadas out of the freezer and cook them for my lunch.

The empanada dough can be made by hand, but it is quicker and easier to prepare in a food processor and it is less likely to become tough from overhandling. If your processor is not large enough to handle three and three-quarter cups flour, make the dough in two batches. Feel free to use a store-bought pie or tart dough to make the recipe even easier (you'll need about two pounds). ✿ **Makes about 40 empanadas**

2 pounds oxtails, cut crosswise into 2-inch pieces

1 carrot, chopped

1 celery stalk, chopped

1 onion, chopped

8 garlic cloves, left whole, plus 1 garlic clove, minced

2 tablespoons black peppercorns

Bouquet garni of 5 or 6 sprigs thyme, 1 bay leaf, and 6 to 8 sprigs flat-leaf parsley wrapped in a cheesecloth sachet or tied with kitchen twine

1 tablespoon olive oil

1 shallot, minced

5 small fresh shiitake mushrooms, stems removed and caps finely chopped

Kosher salt and freshly ground black pepper

⅓ cup dry white wine

In a large saucepan, combine the oxtails, carrot, celery, onion, 8 whole garlic cloves, peppercorns, bouquet garni, and water to cover the oxtails by 2 inches. Bring to a boil, decrease the heat to maintain a simmer, cover, and cook for about 2 hours, or until the oxtails are very tender when pierced with a fork.

Transfer the cooked oxtails to a bowl and let cool just until you can handle them. Discard the broth or strain and reserve for another use. Using your fingers (gloves help protect from the heat), remove the meat from the bones, and discard the bones along with any fat and gristle. You should have about 3 cups (1 pound) meat. Coarsely chop the meat and transfer to a bowl.

Heat a small skillet over medium-high heat. Add the oil and warm it until it ripples. Add the shallot and minced garlic and cook, stirring, for about 2 minutes, or until they are soft but not browned. Stir in the mushrooms and cook for 2 minutes, or until they have softened. Season with salt and pepper, add the wine, and cook for about 3 minutes, or until the wine has evaporated. Remove from the heat, add to the oxtail meat, and stir well. Taste and adjust the seasoning with salt and pepper. Cover and refrigerate for at least 1 hour or up to 1 day before making the empanadas.

To make the mango dip, in a skillet, whisk together the sugar and vinegar. Stir over high heat until the vinegar is boiling and the sugar is melted. Add the mangoes, stir to combine, and decrease the heat to medium. Stir in the *piment d'Espelette*

SPICY MANGO DIP

2 tablespoons dark brown sugar

¼ cup sherry vinegar

2 large mangoes, peeled, pitted, and roughly chopped

1 teaspoon piment d'Espelette (see page 179)

Juice of 1 lemon

Kosher salt

2 tablespoons chopped fresh basil

2 disks Empanada Dough (recipe follows)

2 egg yolks, lightly beaten with 1 tablespoon water

and cook for about 6 minutes, or until the mangoes are soft. Remove from the heat, transfer to a bowl, and mash the mangoes with a fork, leaving them a little chunky. Stir in the lemon juice and salt to taste. Set aside. (The dip can be cooled, covered, and refrigerated for up to 2 days. Bring to room temperature before serving.) Stir in the basil just before serving.

Remove 1 pastry disk from the refrigerator and let it sit at room temperature for at least 15 minutes to make it easier to roll out. (Take the second disk out of the refrigerator to soften just before you begin to roll out the first disk.) On a lightly floured surface, roll out the dough ⅛ inch thick. Using a 3-inch round cookie or biscuit cutter, cut out as many circles as possible. You should have about 20 circles. Gather the scraps and reroll them if necessary to yield what you need. Put the circles on a baking sheet and refrigerate them. Repeat with the second dough disk.

Line a rimmed baking sheet with parchment paper. To fill the empanadas, roll 1 circle a little in one direction so that it becomes slightly oblong. Brush the edges with the egg wash, and mound 1 heaping tablespoon of the filling in the center. Lift a long side of the circle and fold to create a half-moon, pressing the edges to seal. (To make the edges more decorative, you can crimp them like the edge of a pie crust or press them with the tines of a fork.) Repeat until all of the dough circles are filled. Place the empanadas on the prepared baking sheet and refrigerate for at least 30 minutes or up to 2 hours before baking. (At this point, the empanadas can be frozen for up to 2 months.)

Preheat the oven to 375°F. Bake the empanadas for 30 minutes, or until golden brown (bake them straight from the freezer, adding about 15 minutes more time). Transfer to a rack and let cool slightly or to room temperature. Serve with the mango dip alongside.

CONTINUED

EMPANADA DOUGH

✿ **Makes about 2 pounds**

Oxtail Empanadas
with Spicy Mango Dip,
continued

**3¾ cups unbleached
all-purpose flour**

1 tablespoon kosher salt

**1¼ cups (2½ sticks) cold unsalted
butter, cut into ½-inch cubes**

¾ cup ice water

To make the dough, in a food processor, add the flour and salt and pulse a few times to combine. Bury the butter cubes and pulse just until the mixture forms crumbs, with some pea-size (and smaller) pieces. If you do it all in one batch, even a large food processor, you may need to stir up the mixture from the bottom with a spatula (being careful of the blade) to make sure everything is well combined. With the machine running, slowly add ½ cup of the water through the feed tube and pulse until the dough just begins to come together. If the dough is too dry and doesn't come together if you pinch it, pulse in more water, 1 tablespoon at a time, adding no more than ¼ cup. Transfer the dough to a work surface, gather it together, knead it quickly with your hands so it becomes cohesive, and divide it in half. Flatten each half into a 1-inch-thick disk. Wrap well in plastic and refrigerate for at least 1 hour (to allow the gluten to relax) or up to 2 days. The dough can also be frozen for 1 month, and thawed in the refrigerator before use.

TO DRINK

The very hot, dry region of Jumilla is planted primarily with the strong, resilient Monastrell grape, which produces generous, dry, fruity wines. A blend from Jumilla, such as Caracol Serrano, is lush and spicy and a good value, and is a terrific out-of-the-ordinary choice for this mix of buttery pastry and meaty oxtail. **B D F**

BRAISED VEAL SWEETBREADS in MADEIRA

Sweetbreads, which are mild tasting and readily soak up the flavors of other ingredients, seem to have the widest appeal of all the organ meats. They're not difficult to prepare, but if undercooked they'll be too chewy and if overcooked too dry. This recipe has three steps—soaking the sweetbreads, poaching them briefly, and then braising them in wine—which yield perfectly tender, succulent little morsels. I like this preparation for its classic simplicity.   **Serves 4**

1 pound veal sweetbreads

1 tablespoon distilled white vinegar

2 sprigs fresh thyme

1 bay leaf

1½ teaspoons black peppercorns

½ teaspoon kosher salt

2 tablespoons olive oil or grape seed oil

¼ cup ¼-inch-dice carrot

¼ cup ¼-inch-dice celery

¼ cup ¼-inch-dice onion

2 garlic cloves, chopped

1 cup Madeira

½ cup Veal Stock (page 185), Chicken Stock (page 175), or good-quality commercial chicken or veal stock (see Sources)

Bouquet garni of 5 or 6 sprigs thyme, 1 bay leaf, and 6 to 8 sprigs flat-leaf parsley wrapped in a cheesecloth sachet or tied with kitchen twine

Kosher salt and freshly ground black pepper

2 cups loosely packed baby spinach leaves

1 tablespoon unsalted butter

½ teaspoon sherry vinegar

Place the sweetbreads in a bowl with cold water to cover and let soak, changing the water every 20 minutes, for 1 to 2 hours, or until the water is clear. Drain the sweetbreads and place in a medium saucepan with the vinegar, thyme, bay leaf, peppercorns, ½ teaspoon salt, and water to cover by 1 inch. Refill the bowl with ice water, and have it ready near your work surface.

Place the pan over high heat, bring to a boil, and boil for 1 minute. Drain the sweetbreads, discarding the cooking liquid, transfer them to the ice water, and let cool completely. Peel off and discard the membranes from the sweetbreads, and cut the sweetbreads into 1½-inch pieces. Set aside.

Heat a skillet over medium-high heat until hot. Add the olive oil and warm it until it ripples. Add the carrot, celery, onion, and garlic and cook, stirring occasionally, for 4 to 5 minutes, or until the vegetables have softened and are beginning to brown slightly. Add the sweetbreads and cook, turning once, for 2 minutes total, or until browned on both sides. Add the Madeira, bring to a boil, and cook for about 3 minutes, or until reduced by half. Add the stock and bouquet garni, season with salt and pepper, and bring back to a boil. Decrease the heat to maintain a low simmer, cover, and cook for 10 minutes.

Using a slotted spoon, transfer the sweetbreads and vegetables to a plate and discard the bouquet garni. Increase the heat to high and cook until the sauce is reduced to 1½ cups. Strain through a fine-mesh sieve into a glass measuring cup. Let sit for about 5 minutes, or until the fat rises to the surface. Skim off the fat and discard it.

To serve, return the skillet to medium-high heat and add the spinach, sweetbreads, vegetables, and reserved sauce. Stir for about 1 minute, or until the spinach has just begun to wilt. Stir in the butter, allow it to melt, and then add the vinegar. Season with salt and pepper and transfer to a warmed serving platter.

TO DRINK

The trick here is to find a wine that has enough character to handle the opulent veal stock and Madeira, yet possesses enough finesse not to overpower the delicate sweetbreads. The answer is a medium-bodied Tempranillo with some jammy or cherry fruit and a good structure. Try a Montebaco or Gazur from Ribera del Duero. **B D F**

FRITOS
fried bites

ARTICHOKE CHIPS with LEMON AIOLI

A lot of people know that Castroville, California, calls itself the Artichoke Center of the World, but it was news to me when I arrived here many years ago as a young chef. On a drive to Monterey, a friend and I passed through Castroville, where we came upon a restaurant with a huge—about twenty feet in diameter—green sculpture of an artichoke. Naturally, we had to stop and try the kitchen's signature fried artichokes, which were great at the time but not as good as the ones we now make at Bocadillos. These thinly sliced fried artichokes are an unusual and delicious accompaniment to drinks, and are so addictive you had better be prepared to double or triple the recipe. They will disappear as fast as you make them. Unless your knife skills are first-rate, I recommend a mandoline to slice the artichokes. And for all of you trivia buffs: a young woman named Norma Jeane Baker, better known later as Marilyn Monroe, was crowned the first Artichoke Queen of Castroville in 1948. (See photo page 105.) ❧ **Serves 4**

1 lemon, halved

4 very large globe artichokes with 1- to 1½-inch trimmed stems still attached (about 1¼ pounds each)

Peanut or canola oil for deep-frying

Kosher salt

Lemon Aioli (page 172)

Squeeze the juice of the lemon into a large bowl of water and set near your work surface. Working with 1 artichoke at a time and grasping the stems, cut off one-quarter down from the top (the first 2 rows of leaves). Pull off all of the outer leaves until you reach the pale green inner ones. Spread the leaves open and, using a spoon, scrape out and discard the hairy choke. Using a mandoline or sharp knife, cut the artichokes lengthwise into paper-thin slices (some of the slices will include the stem flesh). Drop the slices into the bowl of lemon water.

Fill a deep, heavy casserole or Dutch oven one-third full with oil and heat to 365°F on a deep-frying thermometer, or until a small cube of bread dropped into the oil sizzles, browns, and then stops bubbling within 30 to 40 seconds. (Or use an electric deep-fryer.) Place a paper towel–lined rimmed baking sheet near the stove top.

Drain a few of the artichoke slices and pat dry on a clean kitchen towel. Drop the slices into the hot oil and fry for 3 to 3½ minutes, or until golden brown. Using a slotted spoon, transfer the slices to the towel-lined pan to drain. Cook the remaining artichoke slices the same way, always letting the oil return to 350°F between batches.

Sprinkle the fried artichokes with salt just before serving. If making a double or triple recipe, keep the cooked artichokes warm in a 250°F oven until all of the slices are fried. Serve the chips hot with the aioli for dipping.

TO DRINK

Artichokes are notoriously unfriendly to wine, but a crisp, slightly herbaceous, unoaked Sauvignon Blanc from California will work well here. **M D**

BASQUE FRIES

Topped with a healthy dash of salt and aromatic, spicy *piment d'Espelette*, these potatoes are my Basque version of French fries. In Spanish they're called *patatas bravas*, and are usually cut into chunks or cubes rather than wedges (as in this recipe). I use one teaspoon *piment d'Espelette* here, along with some hot *pimentón*, which makes the potatoes quite spicy, but you can cut back or increase the amount of heat to suit your taste. **Serves 6**

1½ pounds Kennebec, russet, or other good frying potatoes, unpeeled

Peanut or canola oil for deep-frying

1 teaspoon piment d'Espelette (see page 179)

Kosher salt

Pimentón, picante (hot) or dulce (sweet) for finishing (see page 181)

Cut the potatoes lengthwise into wedges about 1 inch thick and 3 to 4 inches long. In a large bowl, cover the potatoes with cold water for at least 4 hours or up overnight.

Drain the potatoes, transfer to a large saucepan, and add cold water to cover by 1 to 2 inches. Bring to a boil, decrease the heat to maintain a simmer, and cook for 8 to 10 minutes, or until tender yet still firm when pierced with a knife. Be careful not to overcook them or they will fall apart when fried. Drain well and pat dry on paper towels.

Fill a deep, heavy casserole or Dutch oven one-third full with oil and heat to 375°F on a deep-frying thermometer, or until a small cube of bread dropped into the oil sizzles, browns, and then stops bubbling within 30 seconds. (Or use a deep-fryer.) Place a paper towel–lined rimmed baking sheet near the stove top.

Preheat the oven to 250°F. Working in batches, drop the potato wedges into the hot oil and cook for 5 to 7 minutes, or until browned and crispy. Using a slotted spoon, transfer the potatoes to the towel-lined pan to drain. Fry the remaining potato wedges the same way, always letting the oil return to 375°F between batches. Keep the cooked potatoes warm in the oven until all the potatoes are cooked.

Put all the cooked potatoes in a bowl and toss with the *piment d'Espelette*, salt, and *pimentón*. Serve hot.

TO DRINK

These fries, spiced with *piment d'Espelette* and *pimentón*, need a racy and floral dry rosé. Rosés made from Garnacha grapes in Navarre are a good choice. **L D F**

CRISPY SHRIMP with PIMENT D'ESPELETTE

The inspiration for this dish came from one of my favorite Chinese techniques, in which shell-on shrimp are stir-fried until crispy and seasoned with dry-roasted salt and Sichuan pepper. Here, in my Basque version, I toss the shrimp with a mixture of salt, *piment d'Espelette*, and smoked paprika and shallow fry them, then serve more of the spice mixture alongside for dipping. Shrimp cooked in their shells have more flavor, but they are messy to shell at the table, so make sure you supply guests with plenty of napkins.

You can use head-on or headless shrimp for this recipe. In either case, make sure they are fresh. It is a little easier to tell with head-on shrimp because the heads go bad first. If they have any black spots or off odors, say "no thanks." By the way, the terms *shrimp* and *prawns* are used interchangeably in fish markets and all that is critical from a consumer's point of view is size called for in the recipe and, more important, freshness. ❧ **Serves 4 to 6**

Peanut or canola oil for shallow frying

¼ cup cornstarch

2 teaspoons plus 1 tablespoon piment d'Espelette (see page 179)

2 teaspoons plus 2 tablespoons kosher salt

2 teaspoons plus 1 tablespoon pimentón, picante (hot) or dulce (sweet) (see page 181)

1 pound large shrimp (about 16), preferably head on

Pour oil to a depth of ½ inch into a large cast-iron skillet or sauté pan and heat to 375°F on a deep-frying thermometer, or until a small cube of bread dropped into the oil sizzles, browns, and then stops bubbling within 30 seconds. (Or use a deep-fryer.) Place a paper towel–lined rimmed baking sheet near the stove top.

While the oil heats, in a bowl, stir together the cornstarch and 2 teaspoons each *piment d'Espelette*, salt, and *pimentón*. Add the shrimp and toss to coat evenly. When the oil is ready, working in small batches, fry the shrimp, turning once, for about 1½ minutes on each side, or until crispy. Using a slotted spoon, transfer to the towel-lined pan to drain. Fry the remaining shrimp the same way, always letting the oil return to 375°F between batches.

To serve, in a small serving bowl or ramekin, stir together the remaining 1 tablespoon *piment d'Espelette*, 2 tablespoons salt, and 1 tablespoon *pimentón*. Arrange the hot shrimp on a platter, with the bowl of salt-and-pepper mixture alongside for dipping.

TO DRINK

Here, we need a wine with some body for the shrimp, but with enough nerve not to be "out-spiced" by the *piment d'Espelette*. Search for a Rueda that is a blend of Verdejo and Viura or Sauvignon Blanc, or both. **M D**

FRIED CALAMARI with ROMESCO SAUCE

Fried calamari is a crowd-pleaser, so I am surprised that few cooks make it at home. Perhaps it is because they think cleaning squid is too time-consuming, or they worry they will overcook it and it will have the texture of rubber bands. This recipe promises to change minds. First, most of the calamari sold today are already cleaned, eliminating that tedious task. Second, if the oil is hot and the calamari don't stay in longer than a couple of minutes max, they will emerge crispy and tender. The classic Catalonian *romesco* sauce is easy to make and is a wonderful alternative to the ubiquitous tomato-ey cocktail sauce usually served with fried calamari. **Serves 6**

Peanut or canola oil for deep-frying

1 cup rice flour

1 pound whole calamari, cleaned (see page 175), or ¾ pound cleaned calamari, whole tubes and tentacles

Kosher salt

Piment d'Espelette (see page 179) for finishing (optional)

Romesco Sauce (page 182)

Fill a deep, heavy casserole or Dutch oven one-third full with oil and heat to 375°F on a deep-frying thermometer, or until a small cube of bread dropped into the oil sizzles, browns, and then stops bubbling within 30 seconds. (Or use an electric deep-fryer.) Place a paper towel–lined rimmed baking sheet near the stove top.

While the oil heats, put the rice flour in a large bowl, add the calamari, and toss to coat evenly. When the oil is hot, put a handful of calamari in a sieve and shake off the excess flour. Tip the calamari from the sieve into the hot oil and fry for 1 to 1½ minutes, or until pale gold. Using a slotted spoon or skimmer, transfer the calamari to the towel-lined pan to drain. Fry the remaining calamari the same way, always letting the oil return to 375°F between batches.

Sprinkle the calamari lightly with salt and *piment d'Espelette*. Serve hot with the sauce for dipping.

TO DRINK

In Catalonia, where *romesco* sauce originated, a Pedro Ximénez dry sherry is served with this dish because it has enough mouthfeel to stand up to the calamari and enough depth not to be trampled by the intense sauce. **B D**

VEGETABLE TEMPURA
with ORANGE SAFFRON AIOLI

The Japanese learned how to make tempura batter from seventeenth-century missionaries from the Iberian Peninsula—the Portuguese—who fried their shrimp and vegetables on fast days when they could not eat meat. Here are three keys to tempura success: First, make sure your oil is clean, rather than recycled. You want to taste the vegetables, not the fat. Second, lumpy batter is light batter. Don't overmix it, and make it right before you are ready to fry. Third, serve the tempura soon after frying. **Serves 4**

⅓ cup rice flour

⅓ cup all-purpose flour

⅓ cup cornstarch

Kosher salt and freshly ground black pepper

Peanut or canola oil for deep-frying

1 cup cold soda water

1 medium-large green or yellow zucchini, sliced on the diagonal ½ inch thick

1 medium-large Japanese eggplant, sliced on the diagonal ½ inch thick

¾ pound asparagus spears, at least ½ inch in diameter, tough ends removed

Orange Saffron Aioli (page 172)

In a bowl, whisk together the rice flour, all-purpose flour, cornstarch, and a healthy sprinkle each of salt and pepper.

Fill a deep, heavy casserole or Dutch oven one-third full with oil and heat to 350°F on a deep-frying thermometer, or until a small cube of bread dropped into the oil sizzles, browns, and then stops bubbling within 60 seconds. (Or use an electric deep-fryer.) Place a paper towel–lined rimmed baking sheet near the stove top.

When the oil is hot, whisk the soda water into the flour mixture until just barely combined. The batter should have lumps. Dip the vegetables, a few at a time, into the batter and drop them into the hot oil. Fry for 4 to 5 minutes, or until golden brown. Using tongs or a slotted spoon, transfer to the towel-lined pan to drain. Fry the remaining vegetables the same way, always letting the oil return to 350°F between batches. If making a double or triple recipe, you can keep the cooked vegetables warm in a 250°F oven until all of them are fried.

Sprinkle the vegetables with salt just before serving. Serve hot with the aioli for dipping.

TO DRINK

Delicately fried tempura vegetables served with aioli call for a wine with good acidity and pleasant fruit tones. In California, Chenin Blanc is the Rodney Dangerfield of whites (it gets no respect), but you will quickly forget that characterization when you try one from Napa Valley's Chappellet Winery or another local winery with this lightly fried dish. **L F**

CHICKEN SKEWERS with YOGURT-MINT DIPPING SAUCE

This Mediterranean-inspired chicken dish quickly became the most popular menu item at Bocadillos. The combination of spiced meatballs and yogurt sauce, reminiscent of great street food, seems to have universal appeal. ❧ **Serves 6**

YOGURT-MINT DIPPING SAUCE

½ cup whole-milk plain yogurt

3 tablespoons finely chopped fresh mint

1 tablespoon sugar

¼ teaspoon piment d'Espelette (see page 179)

2 teaspoons freshly squeezed lemon juice

¼ teaspoon cumin seed

¼ teaspoon coriander seed

¼ teaspoon fennel seed

½ pound boneless, skinless dark chicken meat (from leg and thigh), cut into small pieces

2 tablespoons thinly sliced shallot

1 garlic clove, thinly sliced

½ teaspoon finely chopped fresh thyme

2 or 3 pinches piment d'Espelette (see page 179)

Grated zest of ½ lemon

1 teaspoon kosher salt

1 egg

3 tablespoons homemade fine dry bread crumbs (page 175)

¼ cup canola oil

To make the sauce, in a small bowl, stir together the yogurt, mint, sugar, *piment d'Espelette*, and lemon juice. Cover and refrigerate for up to 1 day. Bring to room temperature before serving.

In a spice grinder, grind the cumin, coriander, and fennel seeds to a fine powder.

In a bowl, combine the chicken, shallot, garlic, thyme, *piment d'Espelette*, lemon zest, salt, and ground spices and stir until loosely combined. Cover and refrigerate for at least 4 hours or up to overnight.

Preheat the oven to 375°F.

In a food processor, combine the chicken mixture, egg, and bread crumbs and process until it is the consistency of coarsely ground meat. Divide the mixture into 6 equal portions. Using your hands, form each portion into a football-shaped meatball about 1 inch thick and 1½ inches long.

Heat a large skillet or sauté pan over medium-high heat until hot. Add the oil and warm it until it ripples. Carefully place the meatballs in the pan, taking care not to crowd them, and cook, turning as needed, for about 4 minutes total, or until lightly browed all over. If the pan fits, slide it into the oven to finish the cooking (if the pan doesn't fit in the oven, transfer the meatballs to a rimmed baking sheet). Bake for 5 to 6 minutes, or until cooked through (making a discreet cut to check).

CONTINUED

**Chicken Skewers
with Yogurt-Mint
Dipping Sauce,**
continued

To serve, have ready 6 small bamboo skewers. Slide each hot meatball lengthwise onto a skewer, and arrange the skewers on a small platter. Accompany with the dipping sauce.

TO DRINK

Priorat in Catalonia is well known for its red wines. But the region's white wines, which make up only 10 percent of the production and are made primarily from white Garnacha grapes, are good food wines when you want something soft (low acid), dry, and full bodied—creamy, even—and that's what works here. **B D**

SERRANO HAM CROQUETTES

Familiar to tapas aficionados throughout Spain, this small-plate recipe is a classic. How can anyone resist the appeal of deep-fried creamy torpedoes of sweet and salty ham? *Croquetas* are endlessly versatile, so you might find them made with ham, cheese, chorizo, or cod. Many chefs like to fool around with them, in the interest of culinary experimentation, but my attitude is why?   **Serves 6**

6 tablespoons unsalted butter

1½ cups all-purpose flour

1½ cups whole or 2-percent milk

5 ounces serrano ham, finely diced (about ⅛ inch)

Generous pinch of kosher salt

2 eggs, lightly beaten

1 cup panko (Japanese bread crumbs) or homemade fine dry bread crumbs (page 175)

Peanut or canola oil for deep-frying

In a small saucepan, melt the butter over medium heat. Add ½ cup of the flour and stir for about 2 minutes, or until combined and foaming. Meanwhile, heat the milk in another saucepan on the stove top over medium heat until small bubbles start to form around the edges (just below the boiling point) and remove from the heat. (Or heat the milk in a microwave oven.) Remove the pan with the butter-flour mixture from the heat and slowly whisk in the hot milk, and then whisk well to remove any lumps. Return the pan to medium-high heat and bring to a boil, continuing to whisk. Cook for 3 minutes, or until the mixture has thickened. Stir in the ham and salt and pour the mixture into a small baking dish or rimmed plate. Spread out evenly, cover loosely with plastic wrap, and let cool to room temperature. Refrigerate for 1 hour.

To make the croquettes, line up 3 shallow bowls on a work surface. Put the remaining 1 cup flour in the first bowl, the beaten eggs in the second, and the panko in the third. Using a spoon, scoop up about 1½ tablespoons of the ham mixture, form it into a log with rounded ends, and place on a plate. Repeat with the rest of the ham mixture; you should have 12 portions. Coat each portion first in the flour, then the eggs, and finally the panko. Arrange the croquettes on a small rimmed baking sheet and refrigerate for at least 30 minutes or up to 4 hours.

CONTINUED

Serrano Ham Croquettes, *continued*

Fill a deep, heavy casserole or Dutch oven one-third full with oil and heat to 365°F on a deep-frying thermometer, or until a small cube of bread dropped into the oil sizzles, browns, and then stops bubbling within 30 to 40 seconds. (Or use an electric deep-fryer.) Place a paper towel–lined rimmed baking sheet near the stove top. Place a wire rack on a rimmed baking sheet, and preheat the oven to 250°F.

Add the croquettes, a few at a time, to the hot oil and fry for 3 or 4 minutes, or until golden brown all over. Using a slotted spoon, transfer them to the towel-lined pan to drain. Then transfer the croquettes to the rack on the baking sheet and keep warm in the oven until all of the croquettes have been fried. Fry the remaining croquettes the same way, always letting the oil return to 365°F between batches.

To serve, place the croquettes on a platter lined with a paper napkin.

TO DRINK

Like a scintillating woman at a dinner party, manzanilla sherry starts out as a quiet guest and then transforms the whole affair into one of grace and beauty (these things can happen to you when you drink great sherry). Seriously, manzanilla is the lightest and driest of all sherries, but it has a pungent and nutty quality that makes it pair particularly well with the meaty flavor of the ham in the croquettes. **L D**

ENSALADAS
salads

SAUTÉED PIMENTS D'ANGLET with BALSAMIC VINEGAR and MANCHEGO CHEESE

The French Basques call them *piments d'anglet*, and vendors in farmers' markets here label them simply Italian frying peppers. These long, narrow, slightly gnarled sweet green peppers are a staple in Basque cooking. I grew up eating them sautéed, but I have taken the recipe a step further by highlighting their sweet flesh with apple and contrasting it with tangy vinegar and salty cheese. Because the peppers are not peeled, look for the smallest ones you can find, no more than six inches long. The skin will be thinner and not as tough. **Serves 4 to 6**

½ cup olive oil

1 small onion, thinly sliced

5 garlic cloves, thinly sliced

1¼ pounds piments d'anglet peppers (see headnote), cored, seeded, and sliced lengthwise into ½- to ¾-inch strips

Kosher salt and freshly ground black pepper

½ cup balsamic vinegar

1 Granny Smith or other tart green apple, unpeeled, halved, cored, and julienned

Small wedge of Manchego cheese

Heat a large sauté pan over medium-high heat until hot. Add the olive oil and warm it until it ripples. Add the onion and garlic and cook, stirring occasionally, for 1 minute. Stir in the peppers, season with salt and pepper, and cook, stirring occasionally, for about 10 minutes, or until the peppers have softened and are beginning to brown. Add the vinegar and ½ cup water, increase the heat to high, and cook for about 8 minutes, or until the liquid has reduced and the peppers are glossy and glazed. Transfer the mixture to a serving platter, taste again for salt and pepper, and let cool to room temperature.

To serve, scatter the julienned apple over the peppers. Using a vegetable peeler, shave thin slices of Manchego over the apples.

TO DRINK
The crisp, apple-y, floral character of one of the many excellent medium-bodied, barrel-fermented California Sauvignon Blancs will mate well with the sweet sautéed peppers, onions, and apples. **M D F**

MUSSELS in RED WINE VINAIGRETTE
with BREAD SALAD

This salad is a longtime favorite with our guests at Piperade. Most bread salads call for stale bread and allow it to soak up the vinaigrette and soften. Here, I add toasted freshly cut croutons just before serving so they stay crunchy, providing a textural contrast to the mussels. I like to use PEI mussels, harvested in the waters off Prince Edward Island, because they are particularly sweet, yet meaty. Look for them in better fish markets and online. ❧ **Serves 4 to 6**

2 tablespoons olive oil

¼ cup minced shallot

3 pounds mussels, preferably PEI (see headnote), scrubbed and debearded if necessary

⅓ cup dry white wine

CROUTONS

3 or 4 slices fine-crumbed bread such as brioche or pain de mie, crusts removed and cut into ⅓-inch cubes

2 teaspoons extra virgin olive oil

RED WINE VINAIGRETTE

⅓ cup minced shallot

1 garlic clove, minced

¼ cup red wine vinegar

⅓ cup extra virgin olive oil

3 tablespoons chopped fresh flat-leaf parsley

3 tablespoons chopped fresh chives

Kosher salt and freshly ground black pepper

2 cups loosely packed frisée leaves

Heat a large sauté pan over high heat until hot. Add the olive oil and warm it until it ripples. Add the shallot and cook, stirring occasionally, for 1 minute. Add the mussels and wine, and cook for 5 minutes, shaking the pan once or twice to redistribute them, until the mussels open. Remove from the heat and let the mussels cool until they can be handled, then extract the mussels from their shells. You should have about 2 cups. Discard any mussels that failed to open. Spread the mussels out on a rimmed baking sheet or large plate and refrigerate for 30 minutes. (You won't need the mussel cooking liquid for this recipe, but it can be saved and frozen, then used to flavor a soup, stew, or risotto.)

To make the croutons, preheat the oven to 350°F. In a small bowl, toss the bread cubes with the olive oil, and spread out on a rimmed baking sheet. Toast in the oven, stirring once or twice, for 10 minutes, or until crispy and golden. Let cool to room temperature. Set aside until ready to serve the salad. (The croutons can be toasted up to 8 hours ahead, cooled, and stored in an airtight container at room temperature.)

To make the vinaigrette, in a small bowl, whisk together the shallot, garlic, vinegar, and olive oil. Transfer the cooled mussels to a bowl and pour over the vinaigrette. Add the parsley and chives and toss to coat evenly. Season to taste with salt and pepper. Refrigerate for at least 30 minutes or up to 8 hours before serving.

CONTINUED

Mussels in Red Wine Vinaigrette with Bread Salad, *continued*

Taste the mussels and adjust the seasoning with salt and pepper. If you'd like to be fancy and serve the salad as shown in the photo on page 121, arrange the mussels on a platter, toss the frisée in a bowl with the vinaigrette and three-fourths of the croutons, then mound the salad in the middle of the mussels. If you'd like a more casual presentation, simply toss the mussels with the salad and vinaigrette. In either case, sprinkle the remaining croutons on top before serving.

TO DRINK

The finest seafood in Spain—maybe even in the world—comes from the northern region of Galicia. Galicians also drink a lot of Albariño wines. That's probably because they marry a vibrant acidity with a mineral quality that suits shellfish ideally. **L D**

ROASTED BEETS with MOROCCAN SPICES and AGED SHERRY VINEGAR

Oven-roasted beets have a sweeter, more intense flavor than boiled beets, and I like to combine them with aged sherry vinegar to enhance their sweetness. You can use any color beet, but if you want to do a mixture, roast the beets separately so the colors don't bleed onto one another. To prevent the beets from staining your hands red, don rubber or latex gloves. Both *ras al hanout*, a Moroccan spice mixture, and *harissa*, a Moroccan red chile paste, are available online and in North African and Middle Eastern markets.

 Serves 4 to 6

2 pounds red beets

1 tablespoon plus ¾ cup canola or grape seed oil

Kosher salt and freshly ground black pepper

¾ cup thinly sliced red onion

¼ cup aged sherry vinegar

1 teaspoon ras al hanout (see Sources)

2 teaspoons ground cumin

1 tablespoon harissa (see Sources)

2 tablespoons chopped fresh chives

Preheat the oven to 400°F.

Trim the stems of the unpeeled beets, leaving 1 inch intact. Rub the beets with 1 tablespoon of the canola oil, sprinkle with salt and pepper, and put them in a small baking dish along with ¼ cup water. (Or wrap them along with the water in a double thickness of heavy-duty aluminum foil.) Cover the baking dish with aluminum foil and roast the beets for 30 minutes to 1 hour, depending on their size, or until they are just tender when pierced with a small knife.

Transfer the beets to a bowl of cold water. When they are still warm but cool enough to handle, top and tail them and slip off the skins. Cut the beets into ½-inch cubes.

In a bowl, combine the beets and onion. In a small bowl, whisk together the vinegar, *ras al hanout*, cumin, and *harissa*. Whisk in the remaining ¾ cup canola oil until combined. Pour the dressing over the beets and onion and toss to coat evenly. Season with salt and pepper. Sprinkle with the chives just before serving.

TO DRINK

A full-bodied rosé will stand up to the beets and the spices. Look to California, where excellent rosés made from Pinot Noir grapes are a good match for this robust salad. **M D F**

SARDINES ESCABECHE

Nowadays, more and more people are ordering fresh sardines in the restaurant, but for years it seemed like I couldn't give them away. Maybe it was because people knew only canned sardines and had no idea how delicious fresh ones are. Or maybe they have just discovered how good omega-3-rich sardines are for us. Whatever the reason, I am now a happy chef because I can sell sardines *escabeche*, which originated as a way to preserve fish and is now enjoyed for its taste. Serve the sardines with shaved fennel or small boiled potatoes alongside.

I am not sure which came first, the demand for fresh sardines or their availability, but I do know that fish markets on both coasts are selling them. Here in California, the once moribund Pacific sardine industry is experiencing a renaissance and you can find the fish in markets from spring to fall, from Oregon to Baja. On the East Coast, European sardines from the Mediterranean are flown in fresh from midsummer to late fall.

 Serves 4

4 fresh sardines (about 1 pound total)

1 small red onion, thinly sliced

1 small carrot, peeled and thinly sliced

3 garlic cloves, left whole

¼ cup dry white wine

1 cup extra virgin olive oil

½ cup sherry vinegar

3 or 4 sprigs thyme

2 bay leaves

1 teaspoon black peppercorns

½ cup unbleached all-purpose flour

Kosher salt and freshly ground black pepper

2 tablespoons olive oil

To clean a sardine, cut off the head and fins and scrape away any scales with the blunt side of the knife. Cut the belly and remove and discard the entrails. Open the fish up by running a finger along the length of the backbone and press lightly to flatten and butterfly it. Lift out the backbone and rinse the fish under cold water. Pat dry with paper towels and set aside while you repeat the procedure with the rest of the sardines.

In a saucepan, combine the onion, carrot, garlic, wine, extra virgin olive oil, vinegar, thyme, bay, and peppercorns and bring to a boil over high heat. Decrease the heat and simmer for 10 minutes. Remove from the heat and set aside while you sauté the fish.

Put the flour in a shallow bowl or pie plate. Sprinkle the sardines with salt and pepper, and then dip in the flour, coating both sides and shaking off the excess. Heat a large skillet or sauté pan over medium-high heat until hot. Add 1 tablespoon of the olive oil and warm it until it ripples. Add 2 of the butterflied sardines (or if you're pan is large enough, all 4) and cook on the first side for 30 seconds. Turn and cook on the second side for 30 seconds to 1 minute, or until the fillets have firmed up. Transfer to a shallow rimmed platter or plate. Heat the remaining 1 tablespoon oil and cook the remaining sardines the same way. Transfer them to the plate. Pour the warm vinegar-vegetable mixture evenly over the sardines. Let cool completely, cover loosely with plastic wrap, and refrigerate for at least 4 hours or preferably overnight.

Serve the sardines chilled with their vinegar and vegetable marinade.

TO DRINK

This dish of strong-flavored sardines combined with vinegar marinade calls for a wine with good acidity. Look no further than a good dry, crisp manzanilla sherry, such as La Gitana from Hidalgo. **L D**

TOMATO and WATERMELON SALAD

If the idea of tomatoes and watermelon together sounds odd to you, this dish will be a revelation. There is a saying that what grows together goes together, and in this case it is true. If you think of tomatoes as a fruit, which they are botanically, this combination makes more sense. Seasonality, however, is the key. I make this salad only in the summer, when tomatoes, watermelon, and cucumbers are at their peak of flavor. Rich, creamy Hass avocadoes are included to lend a nice contrast of flavor and texture. I always toss this salad together before serving, but for the photo opposite I was inspired to create a painstaking mosaic of the ingredients. If you're so inclined, feel free, but don't say I didn't warn you—it takes a lot of time.

 Serves 4 to 6

3 or 4 small to medium heirloom tomatoes, in assorted colors, cored and cut into ¾-inch chunks

1 small English or regular cucumber, peeled, seeded, and cut into ¾-inch cubes

1 cup ¾-inch-cubed yellow or red seedless watermelon flesh

1 Hass avocado, halved, pitted, peeled, and cut into ¾-inch cubes

1 tablespoon chopped mixed fresh herbs, in any combination: basil, tarragon, chives, and cilantro

¼ teaspoon coriander seed

3 tablespoons extra virgin olive oil

3 tablespoons aged balsamic vinegar

Kosher salt and freshly ground black pepper

In a bowl, combine the tomatoes, cucumber, watermelon, avocado, and herbs. In a spice grinder, grind the coriander seeds to a fine powder. Add the ground coriander to the tomato mixture and toss gently.

In a small bowl, whisk together the olive oil, balsamic vinegar, and salt and pepper to taste. Pour over the tomato mixture and toss to coat evenly. Taste and adjust the seasoning before serving.

TO DRINK

If you asked a group of sommeliers which white-wine variety they most often recommend to guests in their restaurants, the majority would answer Riesling, one of the world's greatest wine grapes. Rieslings can vary in style, but all are delicate, acidic, and fruity (often tasting of apricot and peach). Look for a California German-style Riesling that is dry, light, and slightly sweet for serving with this salad, such as the Navarro from Anderson Valley or an Esterlina from Mendocino. **L F**

SNAPPER CEVICHE

I have never lost my taste for marinated raw fish dishes, no matter how ubiquitous they have become on menus, including at Bocadillos. What I try to do, however, is play with the flavors so that diners find something unexpected in addition to the usual Latin American combination of citrus juice, onion, and chiles. Here, in the spirit of the Peruvians—who are masters of restraint when it comes to ceviche—I have added a small amount of fish sauce to give the dish a subtle, slightly Asian nuance.

Any mild, white firm-fleshed fish can stand in for the snapper. If you are using Key limes, you will need to purchase about twenty limes to yield the half cup juice you need. Make sure you don't let the fish marinate longer than fifteen minutes, or it will develop a mushy texture. The ceviche is served atop tomato slices here, a good summertime match. In fall or winter, substitute thinly sliced Fuyu persimmons or Bosc pears for the tomatoes. **Serves 4 to 6**

½ pound skinless snapper fillet, pin bones removed and cut into ½-inch pieces

½ cup freshly squeezed Key lime or regular lime juice

2 teaspoons Vietnamese fish sauce (nuoc mam)

1 teaspoon minced garlic

1 tablespoon thinly sliced shallot

2 or 3 Thai or Serrano chiles, stemmed, seeded, and finely chopped, or more to taste

½ cup coarsely chopped fresh cilantro

1 cup loosely packed inner, pale yellow frisée leaves

1 tablespoon extra virgin olive oil

Kosher salt

1 large ripe heirloom tomato, cored and thinly sliced

In a bowl, combine the fish, lime juice, fish sauce, garlic, shallot, and chiles and toss to coat evenly. Let marinate at room temperature for 10 minutes. Using a slotted spoon, transfer the fish to another bowl and add the cilantro, frisée, olive oil, salt to taste, and 1 tablespoon of the marinade. Toss to combine.

To serve, line a plate with the sliced tomato and mound the ceviche on top.

TO DRINK

The light, slightly effervescent quality of Basque Txacolí is the ideal match for the delicate fish and spicy, citrusy marinade. Txacolí (or Chacolí in Spanish) is a food-friendly wine, particularly with seafood. Not much is exported, however, so Spanish wine and food merchants are the best places to look for it. **L D**

MARINATED BABY OCTOPUS
with TOMATO and FENNEL SALAD

Home cooks typically shy away from octopus, but baby octopus is actually no more difficult to work with than calamari and is cooked in much the same way. Like calamari, it must be either cooked quickly over high heat, or cooked slowly in liquid until it is tender. Many Asian and Latin American fish markets carry fresh and frozen cleaned whole octopuses in all sizes, from baby octopuses that run from fifteen to twenty-five per pound to a single octopus that weighs from one to ten pounds. Fresh octopus is highly perishable, so pass up any specimens with anything stronger than a slight ocean odor. **Serves 4 to 6**

1½ pounds cleaned whole baby octopuses

1 small onion, quartered

1 celery stalk, cut into 2-inch pieces

5 or 6 garlic cloves

Juice of 1 lemon

VINAIGRETTE

2 teaspoons Pernod

⅓ cup tarragon, sherry, or tomato vinegar

1 small garlic clove, minced

1 shallot, minced

⅓ cup extra virgin olive oil

Kosher salt and freshly ground black pepper

1 ripe tomato, cored, halved through the equator, and cut into wedges

1 fennel bulb, halved lengthwise and thinly sliced crosswise on a mandoline

¼ cup loosely packed fresh flat-leaf parsley leaves

Leaves from 2 sprigs tarragon

Put the octopuses in a large saucepan and add the onion, celery, garlic, lemon juice, and water to cover by 2 inches. Bring to a boil over high heat, decrease the heat to maintain a simmer, partially cover, and cook for 45 minutes, or until the octopuses are tender (bite into a tentacle to test). Drain the octopuses, discarding the liquid, and halve lengthwise. Remove and discard the beak and any head matter from each octopus. Spread the octopuses on a rimmed baking sheet or shallow dish.

To make the vinaigrette, in a small bowl, whisk together the Pernod, vinegar, garlic, shallot, olive oil, and salt and pepper to taste. Pour the vinaigrette over the octopuses, cover loosely, and refrigerate for at least 1 hour or up to 6 hours.

To serve, using a slotted spoon, transfer the marinated octopuses to a bowl, add the tomato, fennel, parsley, and tarragon, and toss to mix. Discard the marinade. Season with salt and pepper.

TO DRINK

The vinaigrette and tomatoes served with the octopus call for a wine that has enough acidity to complement the marinade and sufficient lushness to hold up to the octopus. You need a lively, grassy Verdejo-based white from Rueda—the same wine you serve with Black-Eyed Pea Salad with Calamari (page 33). **M D**

BACALAO FRESCO with OYSTERS
and CRÈME FRAÎCHE

In the Bocadillos kitchen, we call this "bacalax" because we cure and thinly slice *bacalao fresco*–fresh Atlantic cod–the same way we do salmon for gravlax. Not only is this an easy and impressive recipe, but it is also a great tapas dish or first course for a dinner party because the fish must be cured for at least six hours, leaving little to do at the last minute. Atlantic cod is available year-round, though it is at its best during fall and winter. Pacific cod is an acceptable substitute for cooks on the West Coast. **Serves 4**

1 pound Atlantic cod fillet
with skin intact

½ cup kosher salt

2 tablespoons sugar

1 teaspoon minced shallot

1 teaspoon freshly squeezed
lemon juice

1 tablespoon crème fraîche,
at room temperature

8 oysters, freshly shucked with
liquor reserved

1 tablespoon minced fresh chives

Freshly ground black pepper

Put the cod fillet, skin side down, on a piece of plastic wrap long enough to wrap the fish. Sprinkle the flesh evenly with the salt and sugar, and fold the plastic up to enclose the fish completely. Refrigerate for at least 6 hours or up to 24 hours.

In a small bowl, whisk together the shallot, lemon juice, and crème fraîche until the mixture is a little foamy. Just before serving, whisk in 2 tablespoons of the oyster liquor.

To serve, remove the cod from the refrigerator and rinse off the salt and sugar. Dry well with paper towels and place on a cutting board. Using a sharp knife, remove and discard the skin from the fillet. With the knife at a 45-degree angle to the cutting surface, slice the fish paper-thin. Arrange the slices on a large platter or on 4 individual plates. (The fish can be sliced and the slices placed between 2 pieces of parchment paper and refrigerated for up to 2 hours in advance of serving.) Place the oysters in the center of the platter, or place 2 oysters in the center of each individual plate. Drizzle the crème fraîche mixture over all and sprinkle with the chives and freshly ground pepper.

TO DRINK

A light, delicate fish, plus oysters (rich) and lemon juice (acid), calls for a white wine with similar characteristics. This dish, like White Bean and Salt Cod Stew with Marinated Guindilla Peppers (page 36) and Chopped Egg Salad with Caper Berries and Fresh Herbs (page 54), calls for a clean and fruity Galician Godello. **M D**

PINTXOS
skewers

BABY BEETS, CUCUMBERS, OLIVES, and FETA SKEWERS

In the restaurant kitchen, I refer to this simple *pintxo* as our skewered salad. Highly versatile, it can be served as part of nearly any large tapas spread, and is especially good alongside Cumin-Scented Lamb Burgers (page 62) or Lamb Loin with Kumquat Chutney (page 28). **Makes 8 skewers**

8 baby beets, about 1 to 1½ inches in diameter

Kosher salt and freshly ground black pepper

8 squares feta cheese, ¾ inch square and ½ inch thick

8 pitted Kalamata olives

8 squares peeled English cucumber, ¾ inch square and ½ inch thick

Extra virgin olive oil for drizzling

Moscatel vinegar reduction (see page 178) for drizzling

Preheat the oven to 400°F.

Trim the stems of the unpeeled beets, leaving ½ inch intact. Sprinkle the beets with salt and pepper, and put them in a small baking dish along with ¼ cup water. (Or wrap them along with the water in a double thickness of heavy-duty aluminum foil.) Roast the beets for 30 minutes, or until they are just tender when pierced with a small knife. Transfer to a bowl of cold water. When they are cool enough to handle, top and tail them and slip off the skins.

To serve, have ready 8 small bamboo skewers. Thread 1 beet, 1 feta square, 1 olive, and 1 cucumber square onto each skewer, and arrange the skewers on a small platter. Drizzle lightly with olive oil and the vinegar reduction. Sprinkle with salt and pepper.

ANCHOVIES with TOMATOES and PARSLEY-DUSTED GARLIC

This *pintxo* is my California interpretation of a classic Basque combination of cured anchovies—*boquerones*—with tomatoes and garlic. Make sure you use fresh, plump garlic cloves that have not sprouted (and are not bitter). **Makes 4 skewers**

8 ripe cherry tomatoes, 1 inch in diameter

1 tablespoon extra virgin olive oil

Kosher salt and freshly ground black pepper

8 plump garlic cloves, peeled

2 tablespoons finely chopped fresh flat-leaf parsley

4 cured boquerones (see page 175)

Preheat the broiler.

Coat the cherry tomatoes with 1 teaspoon of the olive oil, and sprinkle with salt and pepper. Broil for 3 to 5 minutes, or until just barely softened (not falling apart). Remove from the broiler and set aside to cool.

In a small saucepan, combine the garlic cloves with water to cover by 1 inch. Bring to a boil over high heat, decrease the heat to maintain a simmer, and cook for 15 to 20 minutes, or until tender but not falling apart. Drain. Heat a small skillet over medium-high heat until hot. Add 1 teaspoon of the olive oil and warm it until it ripples. Add the garlic and sauté, tossing once or twice, for about 2 minutes, or until golden. Sprinkle with salt and pepper, add 1½ tablespoons of the parsley, and toss to coat the garlic evenly. Remove from the heat and set aside.

To serve, have ready 4 small bamboo skewers. Roll each anchovy fillet into a coil. Thread onto each skewer, in the following order: 1 tomato, 1 anchovy coil, 1 garlic clove, 1 tomato, and 1 garlic clove. Arrange the skewers on a small platter, drizzle with the remaining 1 teaspoon olive oil, and sprinkle with the remaining 1½ teaspoons parsley.

CARAMELIZED ONIONS
with IDIAZÁBAL CHEESE

Idiazábal, a smoked Basque sheep's milk cheese with a tangy, somewhat sweet flavor, has become quite popular in cheese markets. It marries particularly well with the caramelized onions in this recipe.   **Makes 8 skewers**

16 red pearl onions

¼ cup dry sherry

1 tablespoon plus 1 teaspoon sugar

8 squares Idiazábal cheese, 1 inch square and ⅓ inch thick

Piment d'Espelette (see page 179) for finishing

Have ready a small bowl of ice water. Bring a small saucepan filled with water to a boil over high heat, add the onions, and boil for 1 minute. Drain and plunge into the ice water until cool. Cut off the root ends and slip off the skins.

Return the onions to the saucepan and add the sherry, sugar, and water just to cover. Bring to a boil over high heat, decrease the heat to medium, and cook, swirling the pan occasionally, for about 10 minutes, or until the onions are tender when pierced with a small knife and the liquid is syrupy and reduced to 2 to 3 tablespoons. Watch carefully, lowering the heat and adding a little water if necessary to prevent scorching. Using a slotted spoon, transfer the onions to a plate. Reserve the syrup in the pan.

To serve, have ready 8 small bamboo skewers. Thread 1 onion, 1 cheese square, and a second onion onto each skewer, and arrange the skewers on a small platter. Drizzle with the reserved syrup, and sprinkle with a little *piment d'Espelette.*

DEVILED EGGS AND SHRIMP

Deviled eggs are ubiquitous in tapas bars, but in San Sebastián, where *pintxos* have become quite elaborate, you will often see the eggs used as foundations for "skyscrapers" of skewered ingredients. This is my take on that tradition, with poached shrimp and guindilla peppers riding atop the eggs. The trick to getting the skewered eggs and shrimp to stand upright is to shave a little off the bottom of the egg white so it will rest flat. See page 178 for tips on cooking the eggs, and page 137 for a photograph of the finished dish.

 **Makes 8 skewers**

SHRIMP

1 lemon

1 tablespoon red pepper flakes

4 garlic cloves, peeled

Kosher salt

8 large shrimp (about ½ pound total), peeled, with tail segments intact, and deveined

4 hard-cooked eggs (see page 178), peeled

2 tablespoons Aioli (page 172) or mayonnaise

¼ teaspoon piment d'Espelette (see page 179)

¼ teaspoon pimentón (see page 181)

Kosher salt

8 whole guindilla peppers packed in vinegar (see page 179)

Piment d'Espelette for finishing

Fleur de sel or other coarse salt for finishing

Put 2 quarts water in a large saucepan. Cut the lemon in half, squeeze the juice into the water, and add the spent halves. Add the red pepper flakes, garlic, and about 2 tablespoons salt, and bring to a boil over high heat. Add the shrimp and cook for 30 seconds, or until they just begin to turn pink. Drain and set aside.

Cut a thin sliver off of the opposite long sides of each hard-cooked egg, so the stuffed eggs will stand upright. Halve the eggs lengthwise and gently scoop out the yolks into a small bowl. Set the whites aside. Press the yolks through a coarse-mesh sieve or mash them with a fork. Stir in the aioli, ¼ teaspoon *piment d'Espelette*, *pimentón*, and salt to taste. Spoon into a pastry bag fitted with a ½-inch plain or star tip, and pipe the yolk mixture into the whites. Alternatively, use a small spoon to fill the egg-white halves.

To serve, have ready 8 small bamboo skewers. Skewer 1 shrimp and 1 *guindilla* pepper onto each skewer and place on a platter. Sprinkle a little *piment d'Espelette* and *fleur de sel* over all.

SCALLOPS with APPLES

Scallops have a natural sweetness that pairs well with fruit. Also, because they are perfect little medallions of seafood, one or two of them make a terrific appetizer-size portion. See Scallops with Lychee Gazpacho (page 25) for tips on shopping for dry-packed scallops. ✺ **Makes 8 skewers**

7 tablespoons extra virgin olive oil

2 Granny Smith or other tart green apples, peeled, halved, cored, and cut into 1-inch cubes

2 celery stalks

8 dry-packed sea scallops (about ¾ pound)

Kosher salt

½ teaspoon curry powder

Piment d'Espelette (see page 179) for finishing

Heat a sauté pan over high heat until hot. Add 2 tablespoons of the oil and warm it until it ripples. Add the apple cubes and cook for 1 to 2 minutes, or until browned. Using tongs, turn and cook for 1 to 2 minutes, or until browned on the second side. They should be softened slightly but still firm. Transfer to a plate and set the sauté pan aside off the heat.

Have a bowl of ice water ready. Cut the tops and root ends from the celery stalks so the stalks are about 8 inches long. Using a vegetable peeler, remove the strings and cut each stalk on the diagonal into 2-inch pieces. Bring a saucepan filled with water to a boil, add the celery, and cook for 7 to 8 minutes, or until softened but still slightly crisp. Drain and plunge into the ice water to stop the cooking. Drain again and dry with a clean kitchen towel. Return the pan used for the apples to high heat and heat until hot. Add 1 tablespoon of the olive oil and warm it until it ripples. Add the celery and sauté for 1½ to 2 minutes, or until golden. Transfer to the plate with the apples.

In the same pan, heat 1 tablespoon of the oil over medium-high heat until it ripples. Sprinkle the scallops on both sides with salt and add them to the pan. Cook on the first side for 1½ to 2 minutes, or until browned. Using tongs, turn and cook on the second side for 1½ to 2 minutes, or until browned. The scallops should still be slightly translucent in the center. Transfer to the plate with the apples and celery.

To serve, have ready 8 small bamboo skewers. In a small bowl, stir together the remaining 3 tablespoons olive oil and curry powder. Brush the oil over the scallops and apples. Top each scallop with an apple cube and then a celery piece and sprinkle with *piment d'Espelette*. Anchor each vertical stack with a bamboo skewer and arrange on a platter.

SAUSAGE and GUINDILLA PEPPER SKEWERS

Pintxos are small so that you can taste everything together in one or two bites. In this recipe, that means that you will get the bright acidity of the peppers, the sweetness of the onions, and the meatiness of the sausage in a couple of mouthfuls. *Cantimpalitos* are Spanish cocktail sausages, but any high-quality cocktail sausages can be used. 🔹 **Makes 4 skewers**

4 pearl onions

1 tablespoon unsalted butter

1 teaspoon sugar

4 cantimpalitos (see headnote), about 1½ inches long and ½ inch in diameter

1 tablespoon mayonnaise

4 slices baguette, ½ inch thick, lightly toasted

4 whole guindilla peppers packed in vinegar (see page 179) or peperoncini

Have ready a small bowl of ice water. Bring a small saucepan filled with water to a boil over high heat, add the onions, and boil for 1 minute. Drain and plunge into the ice water until cool. Cut off the root ends and slip off the skins.

Rinse the saucepan and return the onions to it along with the butter, sugar, and ½ cup water. Place the pan over medium-high heat, cover, and bring to a boil. Decrease the heat to maintain a simmer and cook for about 10 minutes, or until the onions are tender when pierced with a small knife. Uncover and boil until the water evaporates. The onions will begin to sizzle in the butter remaining in the pan. Continue to cook, turning the onions as needed, for about 5 minutes, or until lightly browned all over. Remove from the heat and keep the onions warm.

In the same saucepan over medium heat, sauté the *cantimpalitos* for about 4 minutes, or until lightly browned on all sides and fully cooked.

To serve, have ready 4 small bamboo skewers. Spread a little mayonnaise on each baguette slice and place on a small platter. Thread 1 *cantimpalito*, 1 onion, and 1 pepper onto each skewer. Place each skewer on a baguette slice. Serve warm.

MONTADITOS
bites on bread

SALT COD with PIPÉRADE

Tapas made with *bacalao* (salt cod) or *pipérade* are common in the Basque region. Here, I have combined the two to create a unique *pintxo*. The purity of flavors calls for seeking out the best-quality salt cod you can find. (See photo page 147.) 🌀 **Makes 8**

2 tablespoons extra virgin olive oil

1 garlic clove, thinly sliced

1 shallot, thinly sliced

½-pound piece salt cod, soaked and drained (see page 182)

1 cup Pipérade (page 181)

Sugar

Kosher salt and freshly ground black pepper

8 diagonally cut baguette slices, about ⅝ inch thick

¼ cup chopped fresh flat-leaf parsley, tossed with a few drops of extra virgin olive oil

Heat a large sauté pan over medium heat until hot. Add the oil and warm it until it ripples. Add the garlic and shallot and sauté for about 2 minutes, or until translucent. Add the salt cod and cook, turning once, for 1 minute on each side. Add ¼ cup water, increase the heat slightly, and cook for about 5 minutes, or until the liquid has almost evaporated and is slightly creamy. Remove the salt cod and set aside.

Drain the *pipérade* in a sieve, pressing out as much liquid as possible. Chop into ¼-inch pieces and put in a small bowl. Stir in a little sugar to intensify the sweetness of the peppers and add salt and pepper to taste (keeping in mind the saltiness of the cod).

To serve, cut the cod into 8 pieces. Mound the *pipérade* on the baguette slices, dividing it evenly. Top each mound with a piece of salt cod and an equal amount of the parsley.

EGGPLANT and AGED GOAT CHEESE

I am picky when it comes to choosing eggplants because they often taste bitter if they are less than perfect. Ideally, they are smooth, shiny, and firm and have no brown spots. This eggplant puree makes more than you will need. You can use the leftover to make a few extra *montaditos*, or you can combine it with some tomatoes and cucumbers for filling a pita sandwich. ✿ **Makes 8**

1 globe eggplant (about 1 pound)

1 garlic clove, thinly sliced

2 tablespoons extra virgin olive oil

2 tablespoons fresh basil leaf chiffonade

Kosher salt and freshly ground black pepper

8 diagonally cut baguette slices, about ⅝ inch thick

5-ounce log aged goat cheese, halved lengthwise and cut crosswise into ⅓-inch-thick half-moons

Piment d'Espelette (see page 179) for finishing

Preheat the oven to 450°F.

Trim off the stem end of the eggplant, and cut the eggplant in half lengthwise. Score the cut side of each half with a 1-inch crosshatch pattern, cutting about ½ inch deep. Insert the garlic slices into the cuts. Place the eggplant halves on a piece of heavy-duty aluminum foil, enclose them in the foil, and transfer to a rimmed baking sheet. Roast for 45 minutes to 1 hour, or until the flesh is very soft.

Remove the eggplant from the oven and unwrap. When the halves are cool enough to handle, scrape the flesh onto a cutting board and discard the skins. Chop the eggplant flesh (along with the garlic) into a rough puree, and put it into a small bowl. Stir in 1 tablespoon of the olive oil and the basil, and season with salt and pepper. The mixture can be served warm or set aside and served at room temperature.

To serve, mound the eggplant puree on the baguette slices, and top each mound with a piece of cheese. Drizzle the cheese with the remaining 1 tablespoon olive oil and sprinkle with the *piment d'Espelette*.

TUNA BELLY with LEMON CONFIT

The beauty of many *pintxos* is that they can be prepared in an instant if you have a can opener and a well-stocked pantry. One item I'm never without is tuna belly, or *ventresca*, which is to tuna what fillet is to beef and foie gras is to geese. Cut from the belly of the albacore (also called *bonito del norte*), it is becoming rarer (and more expensive) because of the high demand for it in Japan, where it is known as *toro*. Incredibly smooth and almost velvety in texture, it should only be used in dishes where it can star. It's available packed in olive oil in cans and jars and is imported from both Spain and Italy, but note that *ventresca* is the Italian word for tuna belly and not all producers use the term.

At the restaurant, we make our own lemon confit, but purchased Moroccan preserved lemons are similar and make a good substitute. **Makes 8**

1 small piquillo pepper
(see page 179)

1 tablespoon capers, rinsed and drained

¼ cup pitted brine-cured black olives, such as Saracena, Amfissa, or Niçoise

¼ cup Aioli (page 172)

8 diagonally cut baguette slices, about ⅝ inch thick

1 (4½-ounce) can tuna belly (ventresca) packed in olive oil, drained and broken into 8 equal pieces (see headnote)

3 tablespoons rind from Confit of Lemon (page 176), sliced in very thin (⅛ inch or less) strips

On a cutting board, finely chop together the *piquillo* pepper, capers, and olives. Transfer to a small bowl, add the aioli, and mix well.

To serve, mound the pepper mixture on the baguette slices, dividing it evenly. Top each mound with a piece of tuna and a little lemon confit.

SEARED BEEF with PIQUILLO PEPPER and SHALLOT JAM

This is a kind of beef carpaccio on bread. It makes a terrific small plate, and you can also gussy it up by toasting the bread slices before you top them and then serving them as hors d'oeuvres with cocktails.

 Makes 8

PIQUILLO PEPPER AND SHALLOT JAM

2 tablespoons extra virgin olive oil

5 garlic cloves, thinly sliced

1 shallot, minced

4 piquillo peppers (see page 179), sliced into ¼-inch strips

½ cup Pedro Ximénez sweet sherry

¼ cup sherry vinegar

½ teaspoon piment d'Espelette (see page 179)

Kosher salt

1 tablespoon olive oil

Kosher salt

Piment d'Espelette (see page 179)

1 piece beef fillet (about ½ pound)

¼ cup Aioli (page 172) or mayonnaise

8 diagonally cut baguette slices, about ⅝ inch thick (or use a biscuit cutter to cut 2½-inch rounds from ⅝-inch thick slices of whole wheat bread)

2 cups arugula leaves, tossed with a little extra virgin olive oil

Heat a small saucepan over medium-high heat. Add the oil and warm it until it ripples. Add the garlic, shallot, and *piquillo* peppers and cook, stirring, for 1 minute. Add the sherry and sherry vinegar and bring to a boil. Decrease the heat to maintain a simmer and cook for 10 to 12 minutes, or until the liquid is almost evaporated. Season with the *piment d'Espelette* and with salt to taste. Remove from the heat and set aside. (The jam can be made up to 5 days ahead, covered, and refrigerated. Bring to room temperature before serving.)

Heat a large sauté pan over medium-high heat until hot. Add the olive oil and warm it until it ripples. Sprinkle salt and *piment d'Espelette* on all sides of the beef filet. Add the meat to the pan and cook on the first side for about 3 minutes, or until browned. Using tongs, turn and cook on the second side for 3 minutes, or until browned. The beef should be rare to medium-rare. Transfer the beef to a cutting board and let rest and cool for at least 30 minutes. (The beef can be cooled completely, covered, and kept at room temperature for up to 4 hours.)

To serve, slice the beef about ¼ inch thick or thinner. You will need a total of 8 slices. Spread a little aioli on the bread slices, dividing it evenly. Roll up each beef slice. Place 1 beef roll on each bread, and top with a little of the jam. Garnish with the arugula or serve it alongside.

SARDINE RILLETTES and PIMIENTOS DE PADRÓN

This simple pâtélike spread of sardines and butter is delicious, but what makes this *montadito* special are the *pimientos de Padrón* served with it. All but unknown outside of Spain until a few years ago, these peppers can often be found fresh at farmers' markets (Happy Quail Farms grows them in California) and on the La Tienda website when they're available (usually in the summer). They are about thumb size, green, and usually sweet, though every so often one can surprise you with its fierce heat. In tapas bars, they are sautéed in olive oil until they blister and then served with a sprinkle of coarse sea salt.   **Makes 8**

2 (4¼ ounces each) cans sardines packed in olive oil, drained

4 tablespoons unsalted butter, at room temperature

Juice of ½ lemon

½ teaspoon piment d'Espelette (see page 179)

Kosher salt

2 tablespoons extra virgin olive oil

8 Padrón peppers (see headnote)

Fleur de sel or other coarse salt for finishing

8 diagonally cut baguette slices, about ⅝ inch thick

In a small bowl, using a fork, mash together the sardines and butter. Add the lemon juice, *piment d'Espelette*, and kosher salt to taste. (Keep in mind that the sardines are salty and will be served with salted *pimientos de Padrón*.)

Heat a small skillet over medium-high heat until hot. Add the olive oil and warm it until it ripples. Add the peppers and cook, turning as needed, for 2 to 3 minutes, or until blistered on all sides. Transfer to a plate and sprinkle with *fleur de sel*.

To serve, mound the sardine mixture on the baguette slices, dividing it evenly. Top each mound with a pepper.

POTATO and CHORIZO BRANDADE

Everyone I have served this tapa to has liked it—and it is nothing more than mashed potatoes and chorizo on bread. What could be simpler? ❧ **Makes 8**

½ **pound dry-cured Spanish chorizo (see page 184)**

1 **pound Yukon gold or other yellow-fleshed potatoes**

2 **tablespoons chopped fresh flat-leaf parsley**

Kosher salt and freshly ground black pepper

8 **diagonally cut baguette slices, about ⅝ inch thick**

Preheat the oven to 450°F.

Divide the chorizo in half. Place the potatoes and half of the chorizo (¼ pound) on a piece of heavy-duty aluminum foil, and enclose them in the foil. Bake for 1 to 1¼ hours, or until the potatoes are tender when pierced with a fork.

Remove the potatoes from the foil and discard the chorizo (it is used for flavor only, and will be too dry to eat). When the potatoes are cool enough to handle, peel them, transfer to a bowl, and mash with a fork.

Cut 3 ounces of the remaining chorizo into ⅛- to ¼-inch dice. Add the diced chorizo and the parsley to the potatoes and stir to mix. Season to taste with salt and pepper.

To serve, very thinly slice the remaining 1 ounce chorizo. Mound the warm potato mixture on the baguette slices, dividing it evenly. Stand 1 or 2 chorizo slices in each mound.

SOPAS

soups

COLD AVOCADO and CILANTRO SOUP

Next time you are looking for something unusual to serve at a summer barbecue, surprise your guests with this soup that I like to call my "liquid guacamole." Smooth, cool, creamy, and rich, it makes a great first course before something off the grill, or at a cocktail party served in demitasse cups. I recommend a stand blender or immersion blender for pureeing soups, which produces a smoother result than a food processor. If you do use a food processor, you will have to strain the soup because part of its appeal is its sublime texture.

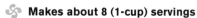 **Makes about 8 (1-cup) servings**

8 garlic cloves, left whole

5 large Hass avocadoes, halved, pitted, and peeled

½ cup freshly squeezed Key lime or regular lime juice

½ bunch cilantro sprigs

2 green jalapeño chiles, stemmed and coarsely chopped, including seeds

Fresh cilantro leaves for garnish

Thinly sliced rings red or green jalapeño chile for garnish

Have ready a small bowl of ice water. Bring a small saucepan filled with water to a boil, add the garlic cloves, decrease the heat to maintain a simmer, and cook for 8 to 10 minutes, or until the garlic is soft. Drain and drop into the ice water to stop the cooking. Drain again.

In a blender or food processor, combine the garlic, avocadoes, lime juice, cilantro sprigs, chopped jalapeños, and 2 cups water and process until the mixture is smooth and very thick. Add water as needed to achieve the consistency of heavy cream. (Depending on the size of your blender or processor, you may need to blend the mixture in 2 batches.)

Transfer the soup to a covered container, straining it through a fine-mesh sieve if you have used a processor. Refrigerate for at least 1 hour or up to 24 hours.

To serve, taste and adjust the seasoning as necessary. Ladle into bowls and garnish with the cilantro leaves and jalapeño rings.

TO DRINK

White Tempranillo grapes from Rioja, such as those used by Viña Ijalba, produce a medium-bodied wine with intense tropical-fruit flavors and refreshing acidity, a perfect partner with the creamy avocado and bracing lime in this sopa. **M D**

WHITE ASPARAGUS VICHYSSOISE

Delicate, tender white asparagus—actually green asparagus that has never seen the light of day (it grows under a blanket of soil)—has long been popular with Europeans, but has only recently begun to be appreciated here. Some of the best white asparagus in the world comes from the Navarre region of northern Spain. For a long time, the only white asparagus I could buy here was imported, but now it is being cultivated in California. Canned white asparagus is good, but if it is the only type you have ever tasted, this soup made with fresh asparagus will be a revelation. It has a fresh, lively, subtle flavor that is reminiscent of hearts of palm or mild artichoke. Look for fat, glossy, pearlescent spears that are not dry at the base.

 Makes about 8 (1-cup) servings

½ cup Pedro Ximénez sweet sherry

½ cup sherry vinegar

2 pounds white asparagus spears

¼ cup extra virgin olive oil

1½ cups diced onion

5 garlic cloves, lightly crushed

6 cups Chicken Stock (page 175) or good-quality commercial chicken stock (see Sources)

½ cup homemade coarse fresh bread crumbs (page 175)

Kosher salt and freshly ground white pepper

Juice of 1 lemon

¼ cup sliced almonds, toasted

In a small saucepan, bring the sherry and sherry vinegar to a boil over medium-high heat. Decrease the heat to medium and cook for about 10 minutes, or until reduced to 2 tablespoons. Remove from the heat and set aside.

Cut off and discard the tough ends and then cut the asparagus into 2-inch pieces. Set aside ½ cup of the asparagus tips for garnish.

Heat a large saucepan over medium heat until hot. Add the oil and warm it until it ripples. Add the onion and garlic and cook, stirring occasionally, for about 6 minutes, or until the onion has softened and is translucent. Stir in the asparagus and pour in the stock. Increase the heat to high, bring to a boil, and then decrease the heat to maintain a simmer. Cover and cook for about 20 minutes. Stir in the bread crumbs and simmer for 10 minutes more, or until the asparagus is very tender.

While the soup is cooking, have ready a small bowl of ice water. Bring a small saucepan filled with water to a boil over high heat. Add the reserved asparagus tips, decrease the heat to a simmer, and cook for 1 to 2 minutes, or until tender but still crisp. Using a slotted spoon, transfer to the ice water to stop the cooking. Drain and set aside.

CONTINUED

**White Asparagus
Vichyssoise,** *continued*

Remove the soup from the heat and let cool for 10 minutes. Process in a stand blender or food processor or with an immersion blender until smooth. (Depending on the size of your blender or processor, you may need to blend the mixture in 2 batches.) Strain through a fine-mesh sieve into a clean saucepan, season to taste with salt and pepper, and add the lemon juice. (At this point, the soup can be cooled, covered, and refrigerated for 2 days.)

To serve, reheat the soup (it cools during pureeing) and ladle into warmed soup bowls. Garnish with the almonds and reserved asparagus tips.

TO DRINK

You must choose a white that is delicate so it won't overwhelm the asparagus, yet has enough structure to hold its own against the tartness of the soup. A dry Palomino table wine would work well. **L D**

COLD MELON SHOOTERS
with SERRANO HAM CRISPS

This soup is all about the flavor of melon. The variety you choose is up to you, but because there are just three main ingredients in the recipe, they all must be perfect. That means the quality of the melon—its ripeness—is nonnegotiable. I like to use Charentais melons, a French heirloom variety that I buy at the local farmers' market in the summer, but cantaloupe, honeydew, Crenshaw, and Canary are also good choices. (See photo page 157.) **Makes 6 to 7 cups; enough for 8 to 10 shooters with plenty left over**

1 (4-pound) or 2 (3-pound) melons, halved, seeded, rind removed, and cut into large cubes (6 to 7 cups)

¼ cup freshly squeezed Key lime or regular lime juice

Kosher salt

Piment d'Espelette (see page 179) for finishing

8 Ham Chips (page 178), about 1 by 3 inches

In a blender or food processor, combine the melon cubes and lime juice and process until the mixture is smooth. (Depending on the size of your blender or processor, you may need to blend the mixture in 2 batches.) Strain through a fine-mesh sieve into a container, and season to taste with salt and *piment d'Espelette*. (Keep in mind that the ham is salty.) You should have 6 to 7 cups. Cover and refrigerate for at least 1 hour or up to 24 hours.

To serve, taste and adjust the seasoning as necessary. Transfer the soup to 8 small glasses or demitasses, and dust each serving with *piment d'Espelette*. (You will have soup left over.) Top each serving with a ham chip.

TO DRINK

A sparkling wine enlivens both the drinker's spirits and whatever he or she is eating. The *cavas* (sparkling wines) made in Catalonia, which are particularly light, bring out the best in this bright soup. D'Abbatis produces a first-rate *cava* that, for the price, will let you celebrate many times over. **L D**

COLD and SPICY TOMATO BROTH
with CHOPPED VEGETABLE SALPIÇON

It was difficult to come up with a name for this cold soup, which is basically diced summer vegetables and pasta floating in the juices extracted from garden-ripe tomatoes. Is it a minestrone? No, because it is not Italian, though it does contain pasta. It is not a gazpacho either, though it seems like a close cousin. What I do know is that it is delicious. *Salpiçon* is a French term for chopped vegetables bound by a sauce, and though I am using it loosely here, I find it comes closest to describing this elegant, savory broth laced with vegetables.

Making the tomato broth base is easy but requires a little patience. You need to process the tomatoes and peppers in a blender until they are pureed, and then let the puree drain, undisturbed, for at least twelve hours to capture the juices. The result will be a beautiful liquid with the essence of tomato.

 Makes about 8 (1-cup) servings

TOMATO BROTH

6 pounds ripe red and yellow tomatoes, cored and cut into 1-inch chunks

1 large red bell pepper, cored, seeded, and cut into 1-inch pieces

1 jalapeño chile, stemmed, seeded, and cut into ½-inch pieces

2 garlic cloves, left whole

Kosher salt and freshly ground black pepper

3 tablespoons olive oil

2 garlic cloves, minced

1 cup ½-inch-dice carrot

1 cup ½-inch-dice fennel

1 cup ½-inch-dice onion

2 teaspoons fresh thyme leaves

1 cup cut-up haricots verts or other green beans (½-inch pieces)

1 cup ½-inch-dice zucchini

1 cup cooked riso pasta or orzo

To make the tomato broth, working in 2 or 3 batches, combine the tomatoes, bell pepper, jalapeño, and whole garlic cloves in a blender or food processor and process until smooth. Line a large sieve with a triple layer of cheesecloth, and set the sieve over a bowl. Make sure the bowl is large enough to collect 2 quarts liquid without the liquid filling the sieve. Pour the pureed vegetables into the sieve and refrigerate for at least 12 hours or up to 24 hours. Do not stir the pureed vegetables at any point.

Heat a large skillet over medium heat until hot. Add the oil and warm it until it ripples. Add the minced garlic, carrot, fennel, onion, and thyme and cook, stirring occasionally, for about 5 minutes, or until the vegetables have softened but have not begun to color. Add the haricots verts and cook, stirring occasionally, for 2 to 3 minutes. Add the zucchini and cook for 2 to 3 minutes longer, or until the zucchini is tender but still crisp. Stir in the cooked pasta and transfer the mixture to a rimmed baking sheet. Spread out evenly to cool. (The vegetables can be covered and refrigerated for up to 4 hours before serving.)

½ cup ½-inch-dice piquillo pepper (see page 179) or roasted red bell pepper (see page 181)

½ cup ½-inch-dice, peeled and seeded ripe Roma tomatoes

OPTIONAL GARNISHES

Shaved Manchego cheese

Chopped fresh herbs such as chives, thyme, savory, basil, and flat-leaf parsley in any combination

Pesto

Romesco Sauce (page 182)

Lemon Aioli (page 172)

To serve, discard the tomato vegetable pulp in the sieve, and season the liquid in the bowl with salt and pepper. In a separate bowl, combine the vegetable-pasta mixture, *piquillo* pepper, and diced tomato and stir to mix. Ladle the tomato broth into 8 soup bowls, and place a spoonful of the vegetable-pasta mixture in each bowl. Top with 1 or 2 of the garnishes.

TO DRINK

The combination of tomatoes, jalapeño chile, garlic, and bell pepper in this soup calls for a crisp, dry, aromatic white wine made from the Pansà Blanca grape in Catalonia's small Alella region. **L D**

DUNGENESS CRAB BISQUE

When I was a kid, I would go to the shore to catch the little crabs that crawled out from the rocks—called *étrilles*, most no larger than a couple of inches—and bring them home in a pail so that my mom could use them in a soup. First, she would sauté them quickly in a hot pan, and then she would add the tiny creatures to her homemade fish broth. She would always set aside a few of the sautéed crabs for us as a reward for our efforts. They were so small we could munch them shell and all and the meat tasted sweet and just faintly of the sea. I am not saying this rich soup is anywhere near what my mom made because it is much more elaborate (though not difficult) and uses Dungeness crab (my favorite), but every time I make it I think about those tiny *étrilles*. **Makes about 8 (1-cup) servings**

CRABS

1 teaspoon fennel seed

1 teaspoon black peppercorns

1 teaspoon coriander seed

1 teaspoon red pepper flakes

1 bay leaf

2 live Dungeness crabs
(about 1 pound each)

5 tablespoons canola or
grape seed oil

Reserved crab shells

¼ cup tomato paste

1 cup dry sherry

1 carrot, peeled and coarsely
chopped

½ fennel bulb, coarsely chopped

½ onion, coarsely chopped

1 stalk lemongrass

6 garlic cloves, left whole

1 star anise pod

1 teaspoon fennel seed

1 teaspoon coriander seed

1 teaspoon red pepper flakes

1 bay leaf

To cook the crabs, in a large stockpot, combine the fennel seed, peppercorns, coriander seed, red pepper flakes, and bay leaf and fill halfway with water. Bring to a boil over high heat and put in the crabs. Cover the pot, bring the liquid back to a simmer, and cook the crabs for 10 minutes. Remove the crabs from the water and let cool, discarding the cooking liquid.

To clean the crabs and extract the meat, place 1 crab, back side down, on a work surface. Pull on the triangular belly flap, lift it away, and set aside. Pull off the back shell and set aside with the belly flap. Remove and discard the spongy gills from the sides and small paddles (mouthlike pieces) from the front of the crab. Twist off the claws and legs, and then crack them, using a small rubber mallet or hammer. Halve the body with a sharp knife. Using a pick or small fork, remove the crabmeat from the body pieces and the claws and legs. Rinse all the shells and set them aside with the back and belly flap shells. Repeat with the remaining crab. You should have about 1½ cups of crabmeat.

To make the soup base, heat a large sauté pan or skillet over high heat until hot. Add 3 tablespoons of the canola oil and warm it until it ripples. Add the reserved crab shells and cook, stirring, for about 5 minutes, or until they are brown-red and brittle. Stir in the tomato paste and cook for about 2 minutes, or until it sticks to the pan and begins to brown. Add the sherry, bring to a boil, and stir to scrape the bottom of the pan. Transfer the contents of the sauté pan to a saucepan.

1 ripe tomato, cored and coarsely chopped

1 cup heavy cream

1 teaspoon piment d'Espelette (see page 179)

Kosher salt

Return the sauté pan to medium-high heat and heat until hot. Add the remaining 2 tablespoons oil and warm it until it ripples. Add the carrot, fennel, onion, lemongrass, and garlic and cook, stirring occasionally, for 4 to 6 minutes, or until the vegetables are golden. Stir in the star anise, fennel seed, coriander seed, red pepper flakes, and bay leaf and cook for 3 minutes more, or until the spices are lightly browned and fragrant. Transfer the contents to the saucepan.

Add the tomato and 2 quarts water to the saucepan, bring to a boil over high heat, and decrease the heat to maintain a simmer. Cook uncovered for 1 hour, skimming occasionally to remove any fat and foam that comes to the surface, to blend the flavors.

Remove from the heat and strain through a fine-mesh sieve into a bowl. Stir in the cream. Process in a stand blender (in 2 batches) or with an immersion blender until smooth. (One note: For safety's sake, if you're using a stand blender, it's best to let the soup base cool for 10 to 15 minutes and then add it in small batches to the jar because of the danger of scalding hot liquid exploding from the top. Also, make sure you leave off the round feed hole and put a kitchen towel over the opening while you're blending.)

To serve, transfer the soup to a saucepan and bring almost to a boil over medium-high heat. Add the crabmeat and remove from the heat. Season with the *piment d'Espelette* and salt to taste. Ladle into warmed soup bowls.

TO DRINK

This soup, which contains both crab and cream and includes a complex and somewhat exotic mixture of spices in the broth, demands a full-bodied, yet dry Alsatian-style Riesling. Claiborne & Churchill from the Edna Valley in San Luis Obispo County will complement all of the elements. **B D F**

BASQUE CLAM CHOWDER

The Basque Country shares the beautiful, rugged Spanish coastline of the Bay of Biscay with the regions of Cantabria, Asturias, and Galicia to the west. Some of the finest seafood in the world is fished here, and I created this clam-rich recipe to echo the kind of *sopa* you might find on a menu in San Sebastián: simple, hearty, and tasting of the essence of the sea and of earthy Basque peppers and potatoes. It is easy to prepare, appreciated by everyone who likes a good chowder, and perfect in tapas-size portions for entertaining or larger portions for a weeknight supper main course. **Makes about 8 (1-cup) servings**

CLAMS

¼ cup extra virgin olive oil

3 garlic cloves, lightly smashed

¼ cup finely diced onion

1 cup dry vermouth or white wine

4 pounds Manila clams, scrubbed

2 tablespoons olive oil

¼ pound salt pork, cut into strips 1 inch long by ¼ inch thick and wide

¾ cup ½-inch-dice onion

6 garlic cloves, lightly smashed

1 red bell pepper, cored, seeded, and cut into ¼-inch dice

1 yellow bell pepper, cored, seeded, and cut into ¼-inch dice

4 cups Chicken Stock (page 175) or good-quality commercial chicken stock (see Sources)

Bouquet garni of 5 or 6 sprigs thyme, 1 bay leaf, and 6 to 8 sprigs flat-leaf parsley wrapped in a cheesecloth sachet or tied with kitchen twine

2½ cups ½-inch-dice, peeled russet potatoes

Kosher salt and freshly ground black pepper

To cook the clams, heat a large casserole or Dutch oven over high heat until hot. Add the extra virgin olive oil and warm it until it ripples. Add the garlic and onion and cook, stirring occasionally, for about 3 minutes, or until lightly colored. Add the vermouth and the clams and cook, uncovered, for 3 to 5 minutes, or until the clams have opened. Remove from the heat. Using a slotted spoon, transfer the clams to a bowl, discarding any that failed to open. Pour the cooking liquid through a fine-mesh sieve lined with cheesecloth into a glass measuring cup. You should have 1 to 1¼ cups. Set the casserole aside. When the clams are cool enough to handle, remove them from their shells and coarsely chop the meats. Set the chopped clams and cooking liquid aside separately.

To make the soup base, return the same casserole to medium-high heat and heat until hot. Add the olive oil and warm it until it ripples. Add the salt pork, onion, and garlic and cook, stirring occasionally, for 3 to 4 minutes, or until the fat has rendered from the salt pork and the onion has begun to color. Add the bell peppers, decrease the heat to medium, and continue to cook, stirring occasionally, for 8 minutes more. Add the reserved clam cooking liquid, stock, and bouquet garni, increase the heat to high, and bring to a boil. Add the potatoes, decrease the heat to maintain a simmer, and cook for about 10 minutes, or until the potatoes are tender. Season to taste with salt and pepper. (At this point, the soup base can be covered and set aside at room temperature for up to 4 hours or refrigerated for up to 2 days.)

To serve, reheat the soup base to a simmer if necessary. Add the reserved clams and remove from the heat. Ladle into warmed soup bowls.

TO DRINK

Look for a full-bodied, low-acid, dry white wine to complement this rich, rustic chowder. A Garnacha Blanca from Priorat, a wine region with designated origin (DO) status that produces mainly reds, is worth the search. **B D**

PANTRY

AIOLI

The quality of the ingredients makes the difference between a rich, fruity, garlicky aioli and a bitter, oily one. Use fresh garlic cloves that show no evidence of a green sprout and good extra virgin olive oil. While some purists claim that the best aioli can only be made the old-fashioned way, with a mortar and pestle, I find that a food processor or blender does an acceptable job, as long as you make the garlic paste by hand.

Makes about 1 cup

2 or 3 garlic cloves, left whole

Kosher salt

1 whole egg or 2 egg yolks

1 cup extra virgin olive oil

With the side of a chef's knife, crush the garlic cloves on a cutting board, and then sprinkle 1 tablespoon of salt over them. Then mince the garlic to a paste, scraping and spreading it a few times with the knife. Transfer the garlic paste to a food processor or blender and add the egg. Add about 2 tablespoons of the olive oil and process for 1 minute. With the motor running, add the remaining oil in droplets until the mixture begins to emulsify. Then add the oil in a fine, steady stream until all of it has been incorporated and the mixture is the consistency of mayonnaise. Transfer to a bowl, taste, and whisk in more salt if needed.

Use immediately, or cover and refrigerate until serving. It will keep for up to 2 days.

Lemon Aioli: Add 1 tablespoon freshly squeezed lemon juice and 1 teaspoon grated lemon zest to the food processor with garlic paste and egg. Proceed as directed.

Orange Saffron Aioli: Soften a pinch of saffron threads in 1 tablespoon hot water for 5 minutes. Add the saffron and its soaking water and the grated zest of 1 orange to the food processor with the garlic paste and egg. Proceed as directed.

BEANS

In the San Francisco Bay Area, cooks look forward each year to late summer, when fresh shelling beans appear in the markets. Most varieties, such as cranberry beans, are purchased in their pods and must be shucked before cooking. Some others, such as black-eyed peas, are usually sold already shelled. These fresh beans do not need to be soaked before cooking and cook much more quickly than dried beans.

Many people make the mistake of thinking that dried beans will keep forever. But they continue to dry during storage, and when you soak and cook older beans, they rehydrate and cook unevenly, with some becoming soft while others remain hard. Look for recently dried beans at farmers' markets. Or seek out beans, preferably organic, sold in bulk from bins at stores with a high turnover, rather than buying bagged beans at supermarkets.

To cook dried beans, first spread them on a rimmed baking sheet and pick out and discard any stones, twigs, or hardened dirt. Then rinse the beans in a colander under cold running water and drain well. Most dried beans, with the exception of lentils and black-eyed peas, are soaked before cooking. Transfer the drained beans to a bowl or glass measuring cup, and add cold water to cover by 2 to 3 inches (or about three times the volume of water to beans). Let sit for at least 6 hours at room temperature or overnight in the refrigerator, and then drain. The beans will have softened and expanded. Some cooks use a quick-soak method— bring to a boil, remove from the heat, cover, and

let sit for 1 hour—but I have found that beans cook better after a long soak.

To cook soaked and drained dried beans, or dried lentils or black-eyed peas, put them in a saucepan with fresh cold water to cover by at least 2 inches. You want a generous amount of water because the beans must move freely in the liquid to cook evenly. Bring the water to a boil, decrease the heat to maintain a gentle simmer, and cook until just before you think the beans are done, adding more water as needed to keep them well covered and stirring occasionally to keep them moving. Although many cooks dispute the long-held notion that salt toughens beans, I still salt the beans after they've softened in the cooking water, about 45 minutes into the process. The best way to determine doneness is to taste a few beans. They should be creamy all the way through. I take the beans off of the heat about 10 minutes before I think they are done and let them cool in their cooking liquid. Once cooled, they should all be uniformly tender and still intact. At this point, the beans can be drained and used in a recipe, or they can be refrigerated in a covered container for up to 2 days.

How long you need to cook dried beans depends on their variety, size, and age. In general, green or brown lentils and black-eyed peas cook in 30 to 45 minutes, small and medium-size beans cook in 45 minutes to 1¼ hours, and larger beans cook in 1 to 1½ hours. Although yields also vary depending on size, ½ pound (about 1 cup) dried beans will yield 2½ to 3 cups cooked.

BOQUERONES

When I call for *boquerones* in a recipe I'm actually referring to *boquerones en vinagre*, or anchovies in vinegar. These mild-flavored white anchovies are prized throughout Spain for their delicacy. Unlike the more familiar salted anchovies, they are not used as an ingredient in cooking. They're sold in cans and you can find them online and in stores that specialize in Spanish products (see Sources).

BREAD CRUMBS

Why use packaged bread crumbs that taste like sawdust when it is easy (and cheaper) to make your own? I use both fresh and dry bread crumbs in my recipes. Start with 1- or 2-day-old French bread. Trim off the crusts and then cut into ¾-inch cubes. For fresh bread crumbs that are still somewhat fluffy, process the cubes in a food processor or blender until they are the texture—fine or coarse— you want. For fine dry crumbs, let the cubes air-dry for 1 hour, or spread them on a rimmed baking sheet and dry them in a 250°F oven for 15 minutes. Then whirl the cubes in the processor or blender until reduced to fine crumbs.

CALAMARI

Most of the calamari (squid) sold in American fish markets are already cleaned, but sometimes you will need to clean them yourself. First, pull the head and tentacles away from the body. The entrails, including the ink sac, should come away with them. Cut off the tentacles just above the eyes and discard the head and entrails. Remove the hard "beak" from the tentacles by squeezing the cut end, and discard it. Set the tentacles aside. Remove the cartilage (it looks like a transparent piece of plastic) from the body and discard it. Rinse the body inside and out under cold running water, flushing it out well. Unless the recipe calls for leaving the mottled gray skin on the body, pull it off with your fingers. Rinse the tentacles and leave them whole. Leave the tentacles and bodies whole or cut as directed in individual recipes. Pat them dry with paper towels before using.

CHICKEN STOCK

Commercial broth, the kind on grocery-store shelves, is great to have on hand to use in a pinch, but if you want a dish to sing, nothing beats using homemade stock. I buy chicken pieces, particularly wings, when they are on sale at the market, and I also try to accumulate carcasses in the freezer. Sometimes I add a few chicken feet or even a halved calf's foot to the pot to give the finished stock more viscosity.

Makes about 3 quarts

4 pounds chicken wings, legs, backs, or carcasses

1 large carrot, cut into 1-inch pieces

2 celery stalks, cut into 1-inch pieces

1 large onion, cut into quarters

Bouquet garni of 2 to 4 sprigs thyme, 1 bay leaf, and 12 sprigs flat-leaf parsley wrapped in cheesecloth or tied with kitchen twine

1 teaspoon black peppercorns

In a stockpot, combine the chicken pieces with water to cover by 3 inches. Bring to a boil over high heat, immediately decrease the heat to maintain a low simmer, and skim off and discard any foam or other impurities that form on the surface. Maintaining a low simmer, add the carrot, celery, onion, bouquet garni, and pepper-corns. Cook uncovered, skimming as needed, for 3 to 4 hours, or until well flavored.

Strain the stock through a fine-mesh sieve into a clean container, let cool completely, and refrigerate until the fat has solidified on the surface (after several hours), at which time the fat will be easier to remove and discard. The stock can be covered and refrigerated for up to 4 days or frozen for up to 2 months. If the stock has been refrigerated, it can then be brought back to a boil, cooled, covered, and refrigerated for 2 days longer.

Dark Chicken Stock: Before putting the chicken pieces in the stockpot, place them in a roasting pan and roast in a 450°F oven for 45 minutes to 1 hour, or until golden brown. Transfer the pieces to the stockpot, and deglaze the roasting pan with a little water on the stove top, adding the contents to the stockpot. Proceed as directed.

CONFIT OF LEMON

This easy-to-make confit is used peel and all and adds a salty, piquant taste to dishes. If you don't have any confit on hand, you can substitute Moroccan preserved lemons, which can be purchased at specialty markets.

10 lemons, quartered lengthwise

2 star anise pods

1 tablespoon coriander seed

1 cup kosher salt

½ cup sugar

Put the lemon quarters in 1 or 2 sterilized jars just large enough to hold them snugly. Add the star anise, coriander seed, salt, and sugar, dividing them equally if using 2 jars. Add boiling water to the jar(s), filling to the rim. Let cool, then cover tightly and turn the jar(s) upside down several times to combine the ingredients. Store at room temperature, turning the jar(s) occasionally, for at least 3 weeks, then (whether opened or not) keep in the refrigerator for up to 4 months.

CRÈME FRAÎCHE

Although crème fraîche has become fairly common in supermarkets and cheese shops, it's easy and less expensive to make your own. Combine 1 cup heavy cream with 1 tablespoon buttermilk and heat in a small saucepan to 85°F on an instant-read thermometer. Put in a jar, cover, and shake, then let sit at room temperature (from 65°F to 85°F) for 24 to 48 hours. Stir and refrigerate for up to 2 weeks.

FRIED SHALLOTS

I call for these crispy shallots as a garnish in White Bean and Salt Cod Stew with Marinated Guindilla Peppers (page 36), but they are also make a delicious garnish for salads, soups, and sautéed vegetable and rice dishes. You can purchase fried shallots in Asian markets, but homemade ones have a better flavor and are easy to make. Thinly slice 4 shallots crosswise and separate the slices into rings. Spread the rings out on a paper towel and let dry at room temperature for 1 hour, tossing them occasionally so they dry evenly. In a skillet, heat the shallot slices and 1 cup canola oil over medium-low heat until the oil begins to bubble. Adjust the heat so the oil bubbles gently, and fry the shallots, stirring occasionally, for about 10 minutes, or until they have just begun to turn golden. They can burn

quickly, so watch carefully to make sure they don't become too dark. Using a slotted spoon, transfer to paper towels to drain and cool completely. They will become crispier as they cool. You should have about 2/3 cup. Store in an airtight container at room temperature for up to 5 days.

GARLIC CHIPS

Slice 3 or 4 large garlic cloves paper-thin lengthwise (there are some nifty, inexpensive garlic slicers on the market that will make quick work of this task). In a small skillet, warm 1/4 cup extra virgin olive oil over medium heat until it ripples. Add the garlic slices and stir. If necessary, tilt the pan to gather the oil and the garlic along one edge so the garlic is immersed in the oil. Cook for 1½ to 2 minutes, or just until the garlic slices are lightly golden. Do not let them brown or they will be bitter. Using a slotted spoon, transfer the garlic to paper towels to drain and cool completely. They will become crispier as they cool. Store in an airtight container at room temperature for up to 3 weeks. The oil can be strained through a fine-mesh sieve and stored in the refrigerator for up to 1 week. Use for sautéing dishes when you want a subtle garlic flavor.

HAM CHIPS AND HAM DUST

Preheat the oven to 225°F. Arrange thinly sliced (about 1/16 inch) *serrano* ham in a single layer on a rimmed baking sheet and bake for 1½ to 2 hours, or until the slices are crisp and thoroughly dried. To test whether the ham is fully dried, let it sit at room temperature for a few minutes; if it breaks rather than bends, it is ready. Let cool completely, then store in an airtight container at room temperature for up to 1 week. To make ham dust, grind the chips to a coarse powder in a food processor. You should have about 1/3 cup dust.

HARD-COOKED EGGS

I'm very fussy about how eggs should be cooked in recipes that call for them to be "hard-cooked." Actually, they must be neither hard nor boiled. Instead, they must be cooked gently to yield a sunny yellow yolk with no trace of green, surrounded by a soft, not rubbery, white. The following method works best for me: Put the eggs in a saucepan with water to cover by 1 to 2 inches, and place over high heat. When the water just begins to bubble vigorously but is not yet roiling, cover the pan and remove it from the heat. Let it sit for 12 minutes, then drain, place under cold running water, and gently tap the eggshells all over on a counter or with the back of a spoon so the cold water can seep inside. Peel away the shells and use the eggs right away, or cover and refrigerate for up to 2 days. I have also found that "older" eggs, ones that have been in your refrigerator for a week or more, are easier to peel. That doesn't matter for recipes where the eggs are chopped, but keep it in mind for when you want nice-looking whole eggs.

MOSCATEL VINEGAR REDUCTION

I like to have this reduction on hand to use in vinaigrettes and to drizzle over finished dishes. Pour Moscatel vinegar into a small saucepan, place over medium-high heat, bring to a boil, decrease the heat to maintain a simmer, and cook until reduced by half. Let cool and store in a tightly covered jar at room temperature; it will keep indefinitely. For more on Moscatel vinegar, see Vinegar, page 185.

OILS

Both the restaurant pantry and my pantry at home are loaded with oils of all kinds: olive, peanut, canola, grape seed, and various nut oils, with olive oil taking up most of the shelf space. I am amazed at how many fantastic olive oils, both imported and domestic, varietals and blends, are available today, when not long ago, the selection was extremely limited. I have a number of favorites, from Spain, Italy, and California, in addition to the label (Arrels) I share with fellow chefs Laurent Manrique and Sylvain Portay, made from olives from our own trees in Catalonia. If you don't already have olive oils you like, you should organize an olive oil tasting with friends and try a variety of different labels.

In general, you will want to use the more delicate, high-quality extra virgin olive oils (made from cold-pressed olives) when you want the flavor of the oil to come through, such as in vinaigrettes or for drizzling on a finished dish, and pure olive oil (a blend of extra virgin or virgin olive oil and refined olive oil), often labeled simply "olive oil," for cooking. In this book, if a recipe calls for "olive oil," use pure olive oil. At Bocadillos and Piperade, we use a commercial blend of 25 percent extra virgin olive oil and 75 percent canola oil (which you can make yourself at home) for general cooking, and grape seed oil for high-heat sautéing because it has a very high smoke point. Nut oils, such as walnut, hazelnut, and almond oil, are used sparingly in vinaigrettes and never for cooking.

OLIVES

Not long ago, only a few varieties of imported olives appeared in the market, mainly Kalamata and Niçoise, but today we have an array of choices.

The two main varieties imported from Spain are the green Manzanillo, which is large, sweet, and mild, and the greenish brown Arbequina, which is small and slightly smoky. You can use any olive you like in the recipes in this book.

PEPPERS

Many types of peppers are cultivated and eaten in Spain, but only a few of them are used in this book, which are discussed here. Look for them in stores that specialize in Spanish food products or online (see Sources).

Piquillo Peppers: Sweet and piquant, these heart-shaped, meaty peppers, which resemble red bell peppers in appearance, are imported from Spain already roasted and peeled and packed into jars and cans. The best *piquillos* come from the town of Lodosa, in southern Navarre. Watch out for inferior peppers imported from other areas. Lately, I have found fresh *piquillos*, identifiable by their pointy ends, at my local farmers' market.

Guindilla Peppers: Also called Basque peppers, these small, slender green peppers are imported from Spain in jars and are packed in white wine vinegar. They are tart and have a moderately spicy bite.

Choricero Peppers: Shaped like an Anaheim chile, *choriceros* are typically dried and used to flavor soups, stews, and sauces. They are a dark reddish brown and have an earthy, slightly smoky flavor.

PIMENT D'ESPELETTE

Many of my recipes call for *piment d'Espelette*, a dried red chile powder from the French Basque region. The chiles are grown only in and around the town of Espelette, in the province of Labourd.

There you will find the small red peppers strung by hand into garlands, hung to dry in the autumn heat, and then dried further in wood-burning ovens before they are ground. This ground chile has a captivatingly complex, yet subtle spicy flavor, and I have found nothing that compares to it. It can be ordered online and is carried in many upscale markets (see Sources). Frankly, there is no substitute.

PIMENTÓN

Ground from peppers smoked over oak fires, Spanish smoked paprika is available in three levels of heat: mild, or *dulce*, bittersweet, or *agridulce*, and hot, *picante*. The best *pimentón* comes from the valley of La Vera, in the region of Extremadura. It is widely available, both online and in specialty stores (see Sources), and lends an incomparable dusky flavor to savory dishes. Although I may suggest a level of heat in my recipes, which *pimentón* you ultimately decide to use is up to you.

PIPÉRADE

Pipérade is basically a stew of sweet peppers and onions and is the quintessential dish of the Basque country.

Makes 3 cups

⅓ cup olive oil

1 small onion, thinly sliced lengthwise

1 red bell pepper, cored, seeded, and cut
    lengthwise into ¼-inch-wide strips

1 yellow bell pepper, cored, seeded, and cut
    lengthwise into ¼-inch-wide strips

6 garlic cloves, crushed or thinly sliced

4 ripe tomatoes, cored and cut into rough
    ¾-inch cubes

Kosher salt

Piment d'Espelette (see page 179)

Heat a large sauté pan over medium-high until hot. Add the olive oil and warm it until it ripples. Add the onion, bell peppers, garlic, and tomatoes and cook, stirring occasionally, for about 10 minutes, or until the vegetables have softened and have begun to color. Remove from the heat and let cool.

Season to taste with salt and *piment d'Espelette* before using, and then use immediately, or store in a tightly covered container in the refrigerator for up to 5 days.

ROASTED PEPPERS

To roast bell or chile peppers, put them directly over a gas flame on the stove top or a charcoal fire or under a broiler close to the heat source and turn them as needed until the skins are blackened and blistered all over. Transfer the blackened peppers to a resealable plastic bag or a bowl covered with plastic wrap and let steam for about 15 minutes, or until the skins have loosened and become cool enough to handle. Core each pepper and then slit it open and place skin side down. Discard any seeds and cut away the white ribs. Turn the peppers over, skin side up; using a knife, scrape off the blackened skins. (Although some cooks hold the peppers under cold running water when removing the skin, which makes it easier, I don't because it rinses away the flavorful juices.) Cut as directed in individual recipes. If you will be using the peppers whole, core them and remove the seeds and ribs without slitting them open, and then scrape away the blackened skins.

ROMESCO SAUCE

This classic Catalonian sauce is a blend of almonds, tomatoes, sweet peppers, onions, and garlic, traditionally pounded together with bread crumbs and olive oil to form an emulsion. It's super versatile and I'm never without it in my fridge. Serve it with grilled meats and poultry or stir it into a vinaigrette.

Makes about 1½ cups

2 plum or Roma tomatoes

2 sweet red bell peppers (about ½ pound total)

1 garlic clove, left whole

2 tablespoons blanched almonds

1 egg yolk

2 tablespoons coarse fresh bread crumbs
  (page 175)

1 cup extra virgin olive oil

2 tablespoons sherry vinegar

Kosher salt and freshly ground black pepper

Preheat the broiler. Place the whole tomatoes and bell peppers on a rimmed baking sheet, place under the broiler as close to the heat source as possible, and broil, turning as necessary, until blackened and blistered on all sides. Transfer the tomatoes and peppers to a bowl, cover with plastic wrap, and let cool. Working over a bowl to catch the juices, pull off the charred skins from the tomatoes and peppers. Core, halve, and seed the tomatoes. Core and seed the peppers. Strain the juices and reserve them for another use.

In a food processor, combine the garlic and almonds and process until finely ground. Add the tomatoes, peppers, and egg yolk and pulse until well mixed. Add the bread crumbs, and with the food processor running, very slowly add the olive oil, allowing the sauce to emulsify. Stir in the vinegar and season to taste with salt and pepper. Use immediately, or store in a tightly covered container in the refrigerator for up to 1 week.

SALT COD

Avoid the salt cod sold in wooden boxes because you cannot be sure of where it originated or from which part of the fish it was cut. The best *bacalao*, or salt cod, comes from Atlantic waters and is sold in Latin American, Spanish, and Italian markets, usually as whole fillets. Ask for pieces cut from the middle or loin, where the meat is thicker and less salty than meat from near the tail. The fillet should be flexible and moist, and never dry or leathery, and it should be almost pure white, rather than yellow or gray.

To rehydrate salt cod for cooking, soak it in a generous amount of cold water to cover in the refrigerator for 24 to 48 hours, changing the water at least 3 or 4 times. The timing will depend on the thickness. Because you don't want to oversoak the fish and remove all of the salt—it should still taste a little briny—check for saltiness every now and again by cutting off a small piece and sautéing it. When the fish is ready, drain it and treat it as if it were fresh: keep it refrigerated and cook it as soon as possible.

SAUSAGES

Morcilla: If you have ever spent time in Spain, you are probably familiar with *morcilla*, or blood sausage. Almost every region has its own version. All of them include pork blood and usually rice, onions, and herbs, but seasoning can range from sweet or hot smoked paprika (*pimentón*) to cinnamon and cloves. Although artisanal *morcillas* are produced throughout Spain (blood sausages from the northern

province of Burgos are considered among the best), you can buy good commercial *morcillas* there and equally good *morcillas* imported from Spain in the United States (see Sources). They are often served in tapas bars, either cut into thick slices and fried in olive oil or as an ingredient in a stew, such as Morcilla in Cider (page 93). I particularly enjoy eating this comforting dish during the colder months. It tastes best made with sweet-spiced *morcillas*, so look for sausages flavored with cinnamon and cloves.

Chorizo: Although the Spanish chorizo I use in this book is a smoked pork sausage seasoned with *pimentón* (see page 181), Spanish chorizo comes in many forms—thick or thin, fresh or dried, smoked or unsmoked, lean or fatty. Mexican chorizo is fresh and contains chiles and vinegar and is more coarsely ground. It's not an acceptable substitute in my recipes. Authentic Spanish chorizo is available online and in stores that specialize in Spanish products.

SERRANO HAM

Until 1997 it was illegal to import *jamón serrano*, or *serrano* ham, into the United States. Today, this salt-cured and air-dried ham, which is similar to Italian prosciutto but sweeter, drier, and "hammier," is widely available in good delicatessens, Spanish food shops, and online (see Sources). I like to buy a large piece (it will keep for several weeks refrigerated) and slice off what I need, plus it ensures that I have the ends for flavoring soups and stews. Spain's finest air-dried ham, *serrano ibérico*, made from the black-coated *ibérico* pig, is now also imported. The best *serrano ibérico* is now made from pigs that eat only acorns, and there is

no better ham in the world. It is so special, it should be served on its own, with no adornment.

SHERRY

The world of Spanish sherry is vast—styles range in color, sweetness, flavor, and alcoholic content—and can be confusing for the consumer, but for everyday drinking and cooking here are some basic guidelines:

One of the great fortified wines, along with Port and Madeira, sherry is made in Andalusia in the Spanish DO region of *Jerez-Xéres-sherry y Manzanilla de Sanlúcar*. Predominantly made from Palomino grapes, often with small amounts of Pedro Ximénez or Moscatel (muscat) added, the wine is produced through a complex system known as the *solera*, in which a new wine is blended in the barrel regularly with wine from older barrels and topped with younger wine. There are primarily two styles: *fino*, which develops a type of yeast called *flor* that makes the wine light in color, delicate, and dry; and *oloroso*, which does not have *flor* and is richer, darker, and fragrant. Three kinds of *fino*-style sherry are *fino*, which is pale to golden in color, very dry, and crisp; *manzanilla*, which is the lightest and most delicate of the three, dry with hints of saltiness; and amontillado, which has lost some of its *flor* and has begun to oxidize so that it is amber in color and has a rich nutty flavor. *Oloroso* sherry ranges from amber to almost dark brown, and has a raisiny-nutty flavor and a higher alcohol content than any of the *fino* styles. Sweetened *olorosos* are called cream sherry. Palo Cortado, a much sought-after sherry, is a rare variation that begins as an amontillado, then evolves into an *oloroso*, retaining the characteristic tanginess of a *fino* and the dark, rich nuttiness of an *oloroso*. Pedro Ximénez, or PX, is an *oloroso* that is blended with Pedro Ximénez grapes so that it is rich, full-bodied, dark, and sweet.

In the recipes in this book I call for both dry (*fino*) sherry and sweet sherry, preferably Pedro Ximénez. Although I personally prefer Spanish sherries, American sherry-style wines are perfectly fine. Cooking sherry is never, ever an acceptable substitute, and although you don't want to use your most expensive, aged sherry, as a general rule—as with all wines for cooking—use something you'd be willing to drink.

VEAL STOCK

Makes about 4 quarts

2 tablespoons canola oil

8 pounds veal knuckle, breast, or neck bones, or a combination

2 large carrots, cut into 1-inch pieces

2 stalks celery, cut into 1-inch pieces

2 large onions, halved

Bouquet garni of 2 to 4 sprigs thyme, 1 bay leaf, and 12 sprigs flat-leaf parsley wrapped in a cheesecloth sachet or tied with kitchen twine

1 tablespoon black peppercorns

Preheat the oven to 450°F.

Add 1 tablespoon of the oil to a large roasting pan and spread out the bones in the pan. Drizzle the remaining 1 tablespoon oil over the bones. Roast for 45 minutes, turning once to ensure even browning. Add the vegetables and continue to roast until the vegetables have browned but not burned, another 45 minutes. (Don't let them scorch or the stock will taste bitter.)

Transfer the bones and vegetables to a stock-pot. Place the roasting pan over a burner on medium-high heat. Deglaze the roasting pan with a little water on the stove top, adding the contents to the stockpot. Add cold water to cover by 5 inches. Bring to a boil over high heat, immediately decrease the heat to maintain a low simmer, and skim off and discard any foam or other impurities that form on the surface. Add the bouquet garni and cook, uncovered, at a very low simmer for 6 to 8 hours, skimming frequently (the more scum you remove during cooking, the clearer the finished stock) and adding more water as necessary to maintain the same level.

Let the stock cool for 10 to 15 minutes, then strain through a fine-mesh sieve into a clean container. Let cool completely, and refrigerate until the fat has solidified on the surface (after several hours), at which time the fat will be easier to remove and discard. The stock can be covered and refrigerated for up to 4 days or frozen for up to 2 months.

VINEGAR

I like vinegar, so I am always on the lookout for new kinds to try. But there are four kinds that I am never without: red wine vinegar, white wine vinegar, sherry vinegar, and Moscatel vinegar. Most of the red and white wine vinegars I use are imported from France. Avoid the bulk generic supermarket brands, which have been made by industrial methods and lack a profound depth of flavor. All of the best wine vinegars are made from top-quality wines, use a traditional natural conversion process (called the

Orléans method, after the place in France where it was perfected), and are barrel aged.

Vinegar made from Spanish sherry is one of the great vinegars of the world. It has a mellow, mildly nutty flavor that is wonderful in vinaigrettes, especially when combined with a little almond or walnut oil. The very best sherry vinegars, or the *reservas*, are aged in a multi-barrel method similar to that used for balsamic, and can rival some of the best balsamics. Although they can be expensive, they're much less expensive than an aged balsamic.

Moscatel (muscat) vinegar, made from the same grape used to make a sweet dessert wine, is a favorite of mine. It is elegant and complex, with hints of stone fruits and honey. To intensify and concentrate its flavor so that it can be used like an aged balsamic vinegar, I cook it down to make a reduction (see page 178). Or you can purchase a *reserva* Moscatel vinegar, aged for 12 years or more, which will deliver an equally intense, yet more refined flavor.

SOURCES

It's not difficult to find the products I call for in my recipes. These days, in addition to upscale food markets, even well stocked supermarkets have begun to carry basic Spanish products such as pimentón, piquillo peppers, sherry vinegar, olive oil, and Spanish cheeses such as manchego. The first two mail order sources in this list specialize in Spanish products and are the most comprehensive.

La Tienda
888-472-1022
www.tienda.com

Comprehensive array of Spanish products including Spanish cheeses, bacalao (salt cod), ventresca tuna, anchovies, sherry vinegar, saffron, peppers, *pimentón*, chorizo, and *piment d'Espelette*

The Spanish Table
510-548-1383
www.spanishtable.com

Spanish products including *jamón serrano*, ventresca tuna, *boquerones*, *bacalao* (salt cod), sherry vinegar, saffron, *pimentón*, peppers, *choricero*, chorizo, morcilla, and *piment d'Espelette* plus books and equipment

In addition to the above two sources, here are a few of my personal favorites for a wide variety of ingredients.

Artisanal Cheese Center
877-944-7848
www.artisanalcheese.com

Large international selection of cheese including many from the Iberian Peninsula, plus books and classes in New York City

Browne Trading Company
800-944-7848
www.browne-trading.com

Wide variety of fresh fish and shellfish including day-boat scallops, mussels, clams, and sardines

Bryan's Fine Foods
415-927-4488
www.bryansfinefoods.com

Aged Midwest beef online as well as a retail fish market in Marin County California

Chef Shop
800-596-0885
www.chefshop.com

Chicken and veal stocks, plus a wide selection of Spanish ingredients

D'Artagnan, Inc.
800-327-8246
www.dartagnan.com

Online source for duck, duck fat, chorizo, cured meats, and duck and veal stock

Dean & Deluca
800-221-7714
www.deandeluca.com

Many Spanish ingredients including *jamón serrano*, as well as Spanish cheeses, wine, spices, and cured meats

Grimaud Farms
800-466-9955
www.grimaud.com

Duck, duck fat

Happy Quail Farms
650-325-0823
www.happyquailfarms.com

Fresh peppers such as *pimientos de padrón* and *piments d'Anglet* sold at farmers markets in the San Francisco Bay Area as well as occasionally at The Spanish Table (see above)

Market Hall Foods
888-952-4005
www.markethallfoods.com

Spanish products such as tuna, chorizo, piquillo peppers, olives, *piment d'Espelette*, and *pimentón*

Monterey Fish Market
510-525-5600
www.webseafood.com

This retail store in Berkeley carries a wide variety of fresh Pacific seafood, and while they do not sell online or ship, their website contains a wealth of information about seafood and sustainability.

Niman Ranch
510-808-0340
www.nimanranch.com

Naturally raised beef, pork, and lamb

Penn Cove Shellfish
360-678-4803
www.penncoveshellfish.com

Mussels, oysters, and clams

Phipps Ranch
650-879-0787
www.phippscountry.com

Dried gigande beans plus a large selection of dried organic shelling beans and legumes, sold online and in California Farmers Markets

Zingermans
888-636-8162
www.zingermans.com

International selection of oils, vinegars, spices, cured meats, cheeses, and olives

ACKNOWLEDGMENTS

I owe a debt of gratitude to the following people who made this book possible:

Lisa Weiss, for her utter kindness, calm nature, and love of good food. Without her motherly leap of faith, this book would still be a pile of notes in my desk drawer.

Robert Petzold—the great debater—a talented and unflappable chef who not only organizes me better than I could ever organize myself, but who always knows when to add the perfect grain of salt.

Emmanuel Kemiji, a truly great friend whose wizardly wine sense gives my food its perfect partner in culinary crime.

Maren Caruso and her team, Christine Wolheim, Kim Kissling, and Stacy Ventura, for the beautiful photos, and to Maren, for her perceptive understanding of what it was I looking for.

My long-time friend and agent, Fred Hill, who has nurtured my literary dreams.

The entire team at Ten Speed Press, in particular Aaron Wehner, for his belief in this project from the beginning, and Clancy Drake, for her superior editing skills and diplomacy.

Sarah Deseran and Penny Wisner, who took those initial steps with me.

My friends and fellow chefs Laurent Manrique and Sylvain Portay, for inspiring me always.

Dan Weiss, for his wine taste buds and his enthusiasm.

The staff at Piperade and Bocadillos, for keeping things humming while I was otherwise occupied with this book.

Adriene Roche, for keeping my books in order.

All the customers who have appreciated my food and supported me through the years at my endeavors in San Francisco.

The Basque community, for instilling the love of cooking into my identity.

Lisa Weiss would also like to thank:

Agent Jane Dystel, for her always great advice.

Cameron Hirigoyen, for her support and friendship and for her call to me on that Sunday afternoon.

Gerald Hirigoyen, the easiest talented guy to work with in the world, not to mention one of the nicest.

INDEX

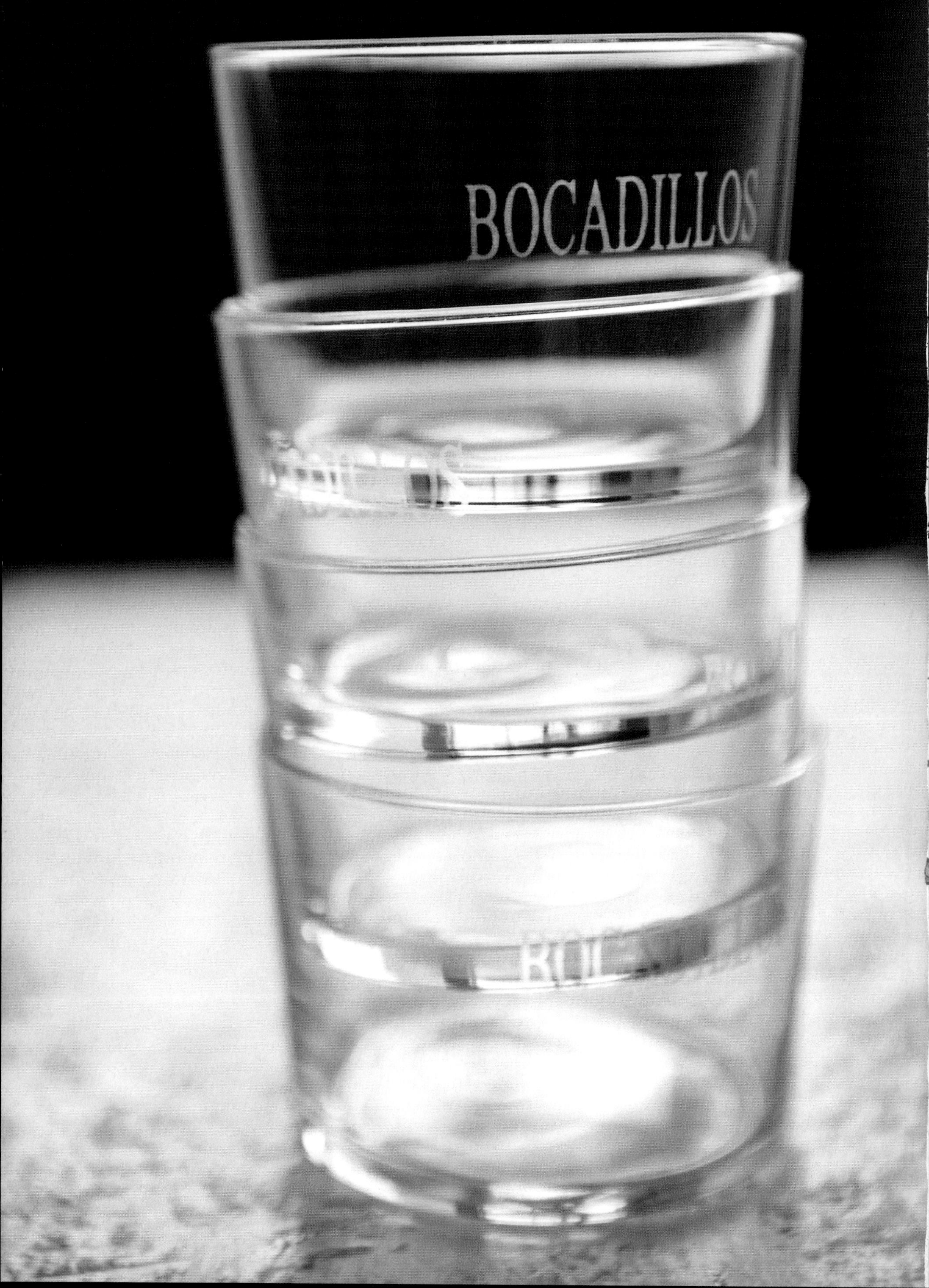
BOCADILLOS